Battle Orders • 24

US Army Infantry Divisions 1944–45

John Sayen

Consultant Editor Dr Duncan Anderson • *Series editors* Marcus Cowper and Nikolai Bogdanovic

First published in Great Britain in 2007 by Osprey Publishing,
Midland House, West Way, Botley, Oxford OX2 0HP United Kingdom
443 Park Avenue South, New York, NY 10016, USA
Email: info@ospreypublishing.com

ISBN 978 1 84603 119 9

Editorial by Ilios Publishing, Oxford, UK (www.iliospublishing.com)
Design: Bounford.com
Index by Alison Worthington
Originated by United Graphics Pte Ltd, Singapore

07 08 09 10 11   10 9 8 7 6 5 4 3 2 1

A CIP catalog record for this book is available from the British Library.

For a catalog of all books published by Osprey Military and Aviation please contact:
Osprey Direct USA, c/o Random House Distribution Center, 400 Hahn Rd,
Westminster, MD 21157 USA
E-mail: info@ospreydirect.com

Osprey Direct UK, P.O. Box 140, Wellingborough, Northants, NN8 2FA, UK
E-mail: info@ospreydirect.co.uk
www.ospreypublishing.com

Image credits and author's note

Unless otherwise indicated, the photographic images that appear
in this work are from the US Army Signal Corps collection. In the
tree diagrams and maps in this volume, the units and movements
of national forces are depicted in the following colors:

US Army units	Olive Drab
German units	Grey
British/Canadian units	Brown
Japanese units	Red

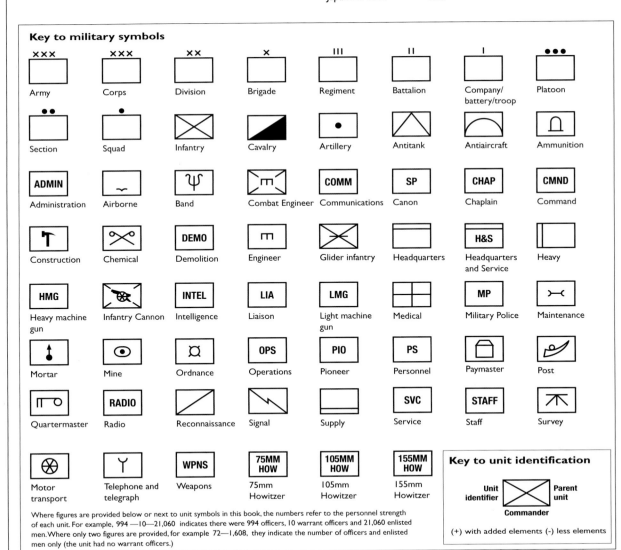

Key to military symbols

Army	Corps	Division	Brigade	Regiment	Battalion	Company/battery/troop	Platoon
Section	Squad	Infantry	Cavalry	Artillery	Antitank	Antiaircraft	Ammunition
Administration	Airborne	Band	Combat Engineer	Communications	Canon	Chaplain	Command
Construction	Chemical	Demolition	Engineer	Glider infantry	Headquarters	Headquarters and Service	Heavy
Heavy machine gun	Infantry Cannon	Intelligence	Liaison	Light machine gun	Medical	Military Police	Maintenance
Mortar	Mine	Ordnance	Operations	Pioneer	Personnel	Paymaster	Post
Quartermaster	Radio	Reconnaissance	Signal	Supply	Service	Staff	Survey
Motor transport	Telephone and telegraph	Weapons	75mm Howitzer	105mm Howitzer	155mm Howitzer		

Key to unit identification

Unit identifier — Parent unit — Commander

(+) with added elements (-) less elements

Where figures are provided below or next to unit symbols in this book, the numbers refer to the personnel strength
of each unit. For example, 994 —10—21,060 indicates there were 994 officers, 10 warrant officers and 21,060 enlisted
men. Where only two figures are provided, for example 72—1,608, they indicate the number of officers and enlisted
men only (the unit had no warrant officers.)

Contents

Introduction

This book, the second of two volumes on the US Army's 66 World War II infantry divisions,[1] covers their history and development from the beginning of 1944 until the end of the war. It was during this period, and especially after the Normandy landings, that most US divisions entered combat. By the end of 1943 the defeat of the Axis powers had become almost inevitable, even though the toughest fighting still lay ahead. In combat, the infantry divisions proved, as before, to be the most useful and versatile fighting arm. Airborne and armored divisions were designed for use in only a limited number of situations, but infantry divisions, when appropriately reinforced, could give an excellent account of themselves against any foe, in any terrain, and in any part of the world. The 19 infantry divisions that deployed to the tropical islands of the Pacific Theater were as effective and useful as the 42 that fought in the plains and forests of France or the eight (of which three later went to France) that served in the mountains of Italy.

Nevertheless, the infantry divisions were heavy consumers of scarce manpower, rubber, gasoline, and other precious resources.

Part of a mortar platoon equipped with the standard M1 81mm mortar firing on the outskirts of Stolberg, Germany, September 19, 1944. Judging from the number of empty ammunition cylinders this platoon seems to have done a good deal of shooting already. A licensed version of a French design, the M1 mortar weighed 136 lb., could be carried by three men, and could fire its 6.87 lb. high-explosive projectiles out to 3,300 yards.

1 The first volume is Battle Orders 17, *US Army Infantry Divisions 1942–43*.

Combat mission and preparation for war

The story of the wartime development of the infantry divisions in the US Army really began in March 1942, when Lieutenant General Leslie J. McNair took command of the newly created Army Ground Forces (AGF). The AGF owed its existence to the influence of the Army Air Corps (AAC), which had caused the War Department to place all Army units not deployed in combat theaters under separate commands for ground (AGF), air (AAF), and service forces (ASF). The new commands assumed all the responsibilities of the existing service branches for training, organization, and doctrine. By grouping all air units under the AAF, the AAC would bring itself a step closer to becoming an independent service.

McNair had been involved in organizational matters since World War I. As a colonel, he had been the chief of staff of the 2d Infantry Division when it field-tested the prototype triangular division in 1936–37. Based on the experience gained from these tests, in March 1938 McNair proposed that the War Department adopt a very austere division of 10,275 troops. Although the War Department largely accepted his recommendations it permitted a series of individually small but cumulatively large manpower increases, which by June of 1941 raised the strength of an infantry division to 15,245. The organization tables for the April 1, 1942 division (discussed in detail in Battle Orders 17) added self-propelled artillery, more and heavier trucks, and 49 more antitank guns, but only 269 more men. McNair had taken over the AGF only a month before this, too late to affect the War Department decision to adopt the new tables.

McNair was one of the few senior American officers in 1942 who understood the need to economize on both manpower (despite the draft) and equipment (despite industrial mobilization). In World War I the War Department designed

Japanese-American troops of the 100th Infantry Battalion, then serving as 1st Battalion, 442nd Infantry, attached to the 34th Infantry Division, line up on both sides of a street in central Livorno, Italy, July 19, 1944.

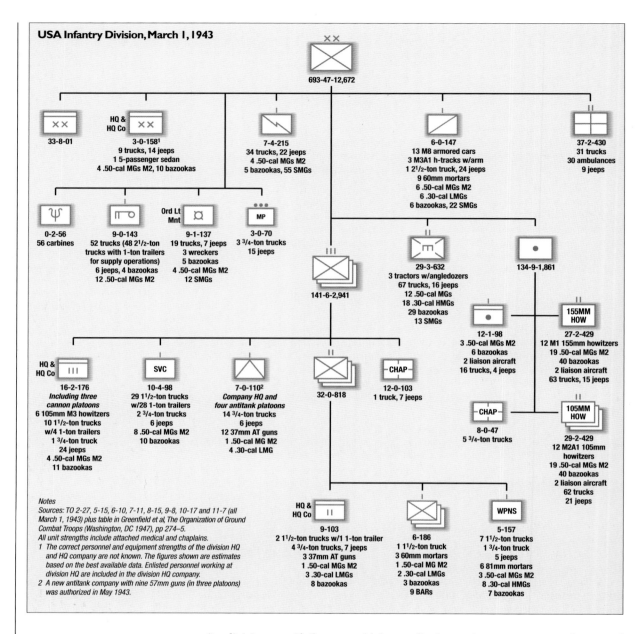

USA Infantry Division, March 1, 1943

XX
693-47-12,672

XX
33-8-01

HQ & HQ Co
XX
3-0-158[1]
9 trucks, 14 jeeps
1 5-passenger sedan
4 .50-cal MGs M2, 10 bazookas

7-4-215
34 trucks, 22 jeeps
4 .50-cal MGs M2
5 bazookas, 55 SMGs

6-0-147
13 M8 armored cars
3 M3A1 h-tracks w/arm
1 2½-ton truck, 24 jeeps
9 60mm mortars
6 .50-cal MGs M2
6 .30-cal LMGs
6 bazookas, 22 SMGs

37-2-430
31 trucks
30 ambulances
9 jeeps

0-2-56
56 carbines

9-0-143
52 trucks (48 2½-ton trucks with 1-ton trailers for supply operations)
6 jeeps, 4 bazookas
12 .50-cal MGs M2

Ord Lt Mnt
9-1-137
19 trucks, 7 jeeps
3 wreckers
5 bazookas
4 .50-cal MGs M2
12 SMGs

MP
3-0-70
3 ¾-ton trucks
15 jeeps

III
141-6-2,941

29-3-632
3 tractors w/angledozers
67 trucks, 16 jeeps
12 .50-cal MGs
18 .30-cal HMGs
29 bazookas
13 SMGs

134-9-1,861

12-1-98
3 .50-cal MGs M2
6 bazookas
2 liaison aircraft
16 trucks, 4 jeeps

155MM HOW
27-2-429
12 M1 155mm howitzers
19 .50-cal MGs M2
40 bazookas
2 liaison aircraft
63 trucks, 15 jeeps

HQ & HQ Co
III
16-2-176
Including three cannon platoons
6 105mm M3 howitzers
10 1½-ton trucks w/4 1-ton trailers
1 ¾-ton truck
24 jeeps
4 .50-cal MGs M2
11 bazookas

SVC
10-4-98
29 1½-ton trucks w/28 1-ton trailers
2 ¾-ton trucks
6 jeeps
8 .50-cal MGs M2
10 bazookas

7-0-110[2]
Company HQ and four antitank platoons
14 ¾-ton trucks
6 jeeps
12 37mm AT guns
1 .50-cal MG M2
4 .30-cal LMG

II
32-0-818

CHAP
12-0-103
1 truck, 7 jeeps

CHAP
8-0-47
5 ¾-ton trucks

105MM HOW
29-2-429
12 M2A1 105mm howitzers
19 .50-cal MGs M2
40 bazookas
2 liaison aircraft
62 trucks
21 jeeps

HQ & HQ Co
II
9-103
2 1½-ton trucks w/1 1-ton trailer
4 ¾-ton trucks, 7 jeeps
3 37mm AT guns
1 .50-cal MGs M2
3 .30-cal LMGs
8 bazookas

6-186
1 1½-ton truck
3 60mm mortars
1 .50-cal MG M2
2 .30-cal LMGs
3 bazookas
9 BARs

WPNS
5-157
7 1½-ton trucks
1 ¾-ton truck
5 jeeps
6 81mm mortars
3 .50-cal MGs M2
8 .30-cal HMGs
7 bazookas

Notes
Sources: TO 2-27, 5-15, 6-10, 7-11, 8-15, 9-8, 10-17 and 11-7 (all March 1, 1943) plus table in Greenfield et al, The Organization of Ground Combat Troops (Washington, DC 1947), pp 274–5.
All unit strengths include attached medical and chaplains.
1 The correct personnel and equipment strengths of the division HQ and HQ company are not known. The figures shown are estimates based on the best available data. Enlisted personnel working at division HQ are included in the division HQ company.
2 A new antitank company with nine 57mm guns (in three platoons) was authorized in May 1943.

---

its divisions as if there would be no limit on the manpower and material available to them. Consequently it could send only 42 divisions to France before the Armistice, and it still had to strip some of these of most of their men in order to fill out the others. For the new war the War Department estimated that it would need at least 100 divisions by the end of 1943, despite the likelihood of much larger diversions of manpower into naval and air forces.

Although the United States was to become the "Arsenal of Democracy" it needed time before the output of its industry could match the needs of the troops. The United States was also exporting large amounts of equipment to its allies. Shortages of strategic materials, especially steel, rubber, and gasoline, placed further constraints on the equipment available. The biggest constraint of all, however, was that no US division would be of any value to the war effort unless it could be shipped overseas – but to do that required cargo ships, and there were never enough of them. Most divisions waited years for their

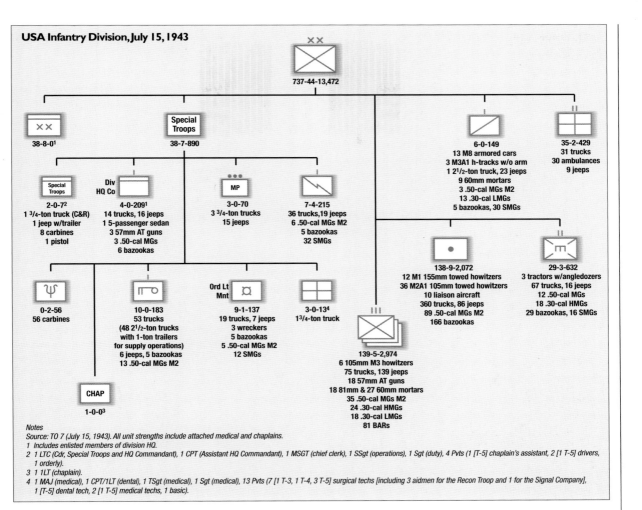

USA Infantry Division, July 15, 1943

737-44-13,472

×× 38-8-0[1]

Special Troops 38-7-890

6-0-149
13 M8 armored cars
3 M3A1 h-tracks w/o arm
1 2¹/₂-ton truck, 23 jeeps
9 60mm mortars
3 .50-cal MGs M2
13 .30-cal LMGs
5 bazookas, 30 SMGs

35-2-429
31 trucks
30 ambulances
9 jeeps

Special Troops
2-0-7[2]
1 ³/₄-ton truck (C&R)
1 jeep w/trailer
8 carbines
1 pistol

Div HQ Co
4-0-209[1]
14 trucks, 16 jeeps
1 5-passenger sedan
3 57mm AT guns
3 .50-cal MGs
6 bazookas

MP
3-0-70
3 ³/₄-ton trucks
15 jeeps

7-4-215
36 trucks,19 jeeps
6 .50-cal MGs M2
5 bazookas
32 SMGs

138-9-2,072
12 M1 155mm towed howitzers
36 M2A1 105mm towed howitzers
10 liaison aircraft
360 trucks, 86 jeeps
89 .50-cal MGs M2
166 bazookas

29-3-632
3 tractors w/angledozers
67 trucks, 16 jeeps
12 .50-cal MGs
18 .30-cal HMGs
29 bazookas, 16 SMGs

0-2-56
56 carbines

10-0-183
53 trucks
(48 2¹/₂-ton trucks
with 1-ton trailers
for supply operations)
6 jeeps, 5 bazookas
13 .50-cal MGs M2

Ord Lt Mnt
9-1-137
19 trucks, 7 jeeps
3 wreckers
5 bazookas
5 .50-cal MGs M2
12 SMGs

3-0-13[4]
1³/₄-ton truck

139-5-2,974
6 105mm M3 howitzers
75 trucks, 139 jeeps
18 57mm AT guns
18 81mm & 27 60mm mortars
35 .50-cal MGs M2
24 .30-cal HMGs
18 .30-cal LMGs
81 BARs

CHAP
1-0-0[3]

Notes
Source: TO 7 (July 15, 1943). All unit strengths include attached medical and chaplains.
1 Includes enlisted members of division HQ.
2 1 LTC (Cdr, Special Troops and HQ Commandant), 1 CPT (Assistant HQ Commandant), 1 MSGT (chief clerk), 1 SSgt (operations), 1 Sgt (duty), 4 Pvts (1 [T-5] chaplain's assistant, 2 [T-5] drivers, 1 orderly).
3 1 1LT (chaplain).
4 1 MAJ (medical), 1 CPT/1LT (dental), 1 TSgt (medical), 1 Sgt (medical), 13 Pvts (7 [1 T-3, 1 T-4, 3 T-5] surgical techs [including 3 aidmen for the Recon Troop and 1 for the Signal Company], 1 [T-5] dental tech, 2 [1 T-5] medical techs, 1 basic).

shipping. Therefore, McNair reasoned that an infantry division had to use as few men and strategic materials as possible and minimize the number of cubic feet it could fit into. In the light of these considerations McNair found the April 1942 infantry division inexcusably extravagant.

McNair concluded that the only long-term solution was to rewrite the infantry division organization tables to make them as "lean" as possible. To do this, he established the AGF Reduction Board. The "no-men," as the members of the board came to be called, reviewed and modified all ground force tables of organization to achieve reductions of 15 percent in personnel and 20 percent in motor vehicles, but without cutting combat effectiveness. McNair personally participated in the work of the board and became the biggest "no-man" of all, often saying "no" to his own "no-men." The "no-men" slashed the proportion of orderlies to officers, gave as many light truck drivers as possible additional duties such as working in the kitchens, and eliminated "luxury" items. Company headquarters lost their tents and were allowed only one portable typewriter each. No chairs, safes, or tables were allowed in any headquarters below division level. The "no-men" assigned all personnel and equipment to specific vehicles and permitted no "reserves." They also increased the use of trailers since these considerably extended the payload of the available trucks. Though leaving all "offensive" weapons in place, they slashed anything whose main function was to increase self-sufficiency in security or supply.

Table 1: Infantry division officer rank abbreviations (1942–43)

Rank	Abbr.
Major general	MG
Brigadier general	BG
Colonel	COL
Lieutenant colonel	LTC
Major	MAJ
Captain	CPT
First lieutenant	1LT
Second lieutenant	2LT
Warrant officer	WO

In particular, McNair tried to discourage what he called "empire building" or the tendency of every arm and service to augment itself as if it had to win the war alone. An example was the persistent demands by many division commanders for their own tank, tank destroyer, antiaircraft, reconnaissance, and military police battalions so they could handle every contingency, not just the ones most likely to occur. There was also the tendency, deeply rooted in American society, to encumber the military with comforts, conveniences, gadgets, technicians, "experts," special services, and complex command–control systems. Naturally, once these additions got started, they multiplied exponentially. For example, if one wanted to increase the number of dentists in a division one would also have to increase the number of dental technicians. Dentists and technicians had to be fed and required more cooks. Cooks, dentists, and technicians needed trucks and their drivers and mechanics. Cooks, dentists, technicians, drivers, and mechanics needed medical care and that meant doctors, nurses, and medical technicians. The cooks, dentists, technicians, drivers, mechanics, doctors, nurses, and so forth needed clothing and that meant more quartermasters – and of course they all needed dental care, which again increased the requirement for dentists. McNair was determined to nip such expansion in the bud.

The "no-men" uniformly observed certain principles. First, for local air defense they replaced all Browning Automatic Rifles (BARs) outside the rifle squads with smaller numbers of much more effective M2 .50-caliber machine guns. Second, they replaced about 40 percent of the antitank guns in a division with large numbers of the new 2.36in. antitank rocket launcher M1 or "bazooka." Neither the bazookas nor most of the .50-caliber machine guns had assigned gunners. Company commanders were expected to train a sufficient number of their men to operate these weapons as an additional duty. Third, in addition to cutting the number of motor vehicles the "no-men" replaced heavier vehicles with lighter ones. In the infantry regiments they used $1\frac{1}{2}$-ton

Infantrymen cross a blown-up bridge over the Marne at Mareuil-sur-Ay on August 30, 1944. German troops dynamited the bridge before abandoning the town.

trucks (with trailers) to replace 2^1/$_2$-tonners on a "one for one" basis or jeeps (with trailers) on a "one for two" basis. This saved fuel and rubber as well as drivers and mechanics.

Not even medical units escaped the "no-men." They cut the number of medical aidmen from three to two per rifle or weapons company, and they required stretcher-bearers to double as drivers, eliminating most full-time drivers.

The "no-men" spared those elements of the infantry that served closest to the enemy from any significant cuts. The rifle and weapons companies stayed largely intact except for the replacement of their jeep weapons carriers with half as many 1^1/$_2$-ton trucks.

At the regimental level, the "no-men" dropped the mine platoon from the antitank company and replaced the cannon company with three cannon platoons in the regimental headquarters company. The cannon platoons would use towed M3 105mm howitzers recently developed for airborne use. They weighed only half as much as the M2A1 105mm howitzers found in the division artillery. An M3 could only range to 8,000m but McNair was confident that it was at least as effective as the ungainly self-propelled weapons it would replace.

Elsewhere in the division the artillery lost its battalion defense platoons and a quarter of its 2^1/$_2$-ton trucks. The engineers lost their armored half-tracks and antitank guns, the quartermaster company lost its service platoon, the division signal company lost its radio intelligence platoon and the division headquarters company its defense platoon. A liaison section from the medical battalion replaced the division headquarters medical section.

The results of the "no-men's" handiwork appeared in March 1943 to a chorus of shrieks, howls, and less printable protestations as every commander saw his own ox gored far more than he thought fair. Chief among the protestors was European Theater commander General Dwight D. Eisenhower.

Army Chief of Staff General George C. Marshall, however, supported McNair. In September 1942 he noted that "if we gave each theater commander what he asked for (rather than allocating resources based on overall requirements) we would have only one theater and all the rest would have to be evacuated for lack of means."

Nevertheless, Eisenhower's influence was strong and McNair's was weakened by the fact that he had been wounded while on an inspection tour in North Africa. This cost him the opportunity to make his case fully. Eventually the parties reached a compromise under which the infantry division would regain about 800 men. In the infantry regiments, the rifle and weapons companies got their jeeps back and the infantry regimental service companies recovered their 2^1/$_2$-ton trucks. The antitank companies got their mine platoons and the cannon platoons became a regimental cannon company again. Outside the infantry regiments the artillery battalions reverted to having separate headquarters and service batteries rather than a combined headquarters and service battery. The division headquarters regained its medical section, the quartermaster company its service platoon, and the division headquarters company its defense platoon. Over McNair's strenuous protests the War Department added a small headquarters to command the division "special troops" – the headquarters, ordnance, quartermaster and signal companies, and the military police platoon – even though all the "special" units operated independently of each other. Even the extravagant April 1942 division had no such headquarters, but it had been used in earlier divisions.

The War Department published the new tables on July 15, 1943 and never implemented the March 1, 1943 tables. However, even the "fattened up" July tables saved enough men for five or six new divisions. As the war continued even field commanders grudgingly came to admit the need for economy. Despite McNair's accidental death in an American air strike as he toured Normandy in August 1944, no one undid his work until after the war was safely over.

Unit organization

The rifle squad

The first significant change to the US Army rifle squad after April 1942 was the late 1943 introduction of the M7 rifle grenade launcher. There was also a similar M8 grenade launcher for M1 carbines. The M7 could be attached to a standard M1 Garand rifle. This allowed each squad to replace its slower firing, bolt-action M1903 Springfield and M1 grenade launcher. Attaching an M7 grenade launcher prevented an M1 rifle from using semi-automatic fire, but the improved M7A1 that appeared in 1944 corrected this. Since any M1 rifle could carry an M7 series launcher, each rifle squad had three. Like the M1 launcher, an M7 could fire M9 antitank as well as fragmentation grenades.

An "unofficial" change was the proliferation of Browning Automatic Rifles (BARs) within the rifle squads. Combat experience had demonstrated the value of automatic firepower, but a single BAR was inadequate for a full squad. Most squads that had seen any combat obtained a second and sometimes a third BAR so that they would have the automatic weapons they needed.

In February 1944 the Army sought to improve its rifle squads' performance by increasing squad leader rank from sergeant to staff sergeant. Assistant squad leaders (and weapons platoon squad leaders) rose from corporal to sergeant. This created a need for an intermediate rank between staff sergeant squad leaders and company first sergeants so that platoon sergeants could always outrank the squad leaders. To meet this need the Army used the rank of technical sergeant, which had previously been a special rank awarded to technicians (see Table 2 on page 11). After February 1944 any NCO could hold this rank. The increase in NCO rank probably produced no increase in quality since the same people continued to do the same jobs, but it did mean faster promotion for enlisted men.

US infantrymen fire their M1 rifles at German snipers from their foxhole built into the side of a dyke, November 1, 1944. Both men have dropped their packs. The cartridge cases ejected from their M1 rifles are clearly visible. An SCR-536 radio sits in the foreground.

The rifle platoon and company

In each rifle platoon one rifleman (chosen by the platoon leader) served as a sniper. He carried either a bolt action M1903A4 (with scope) or the M1C, the sniper version of the M1.

Table 2: Infantry division enlisted ranks

Pay grade	"Hard stripe" rank	Technician rank
1	Master sergeant (MSgt)	T-1
2	Technical sergeant (TSgt)	T-2
3	Staff sergeant (SSgt)	T-3
4	Sergeant (Sgt)	T-4
5	Corporal (Cpl)	T-5
6	Private 1st class (PFC /Pvt.)	None
7	Private (Pvt.)	None
None	Sergeant major (SgtMaj)	None
None	First sergeant (1stSgt)	None

Note: Technicians were paid as NCOs of the same pay grade, but only ranked as privates.

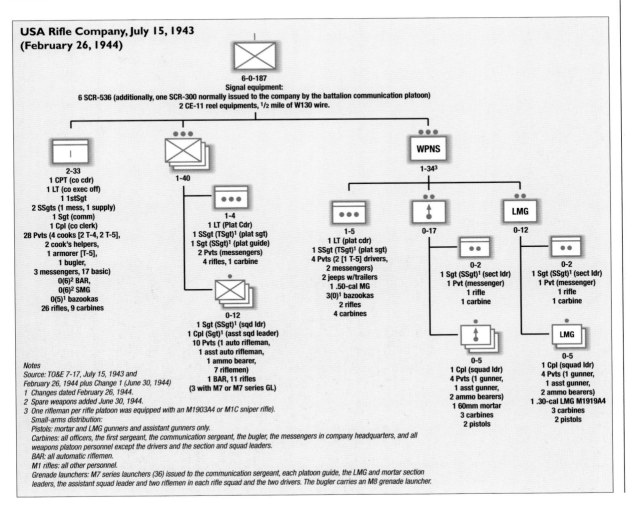

USA Rifle Company, July 15, 1943 (February 26, 1944)

6-0-187
Signal equipment:
6 SCR-536 (additionally, one SCR-300 normally issued to the company by the battalion communication platoon)
2 CE-11 reel equipments, 1/2 mile of W130 wire.

2-33
1 CPT (co cdr)
1 LT (co exec off)
1 1stSgt
2 SSgts (1 mess, 1 supply)
1 Sgt (comm)
1 Cpl (co clerk)
28 Pvts (4 cooks [2 T-4, 2 T-5],
2 cook's helpers,
1 armorer [T-5],
1 bugler,
3 messengers, 17 basic)
0(6)[2] BAR,
0(6)[2] SMG
0(5)[1] bazookas
26 rifles, 9 carbines

1-40

1-4
1 LT (Plat Cdr)
1 SSgt (TSgt)[1] (plat sgt)
1 Sgt (SSgt)[1] (plat guide)
2 Pvts (messengers)
4 rifles, 1 carbine

0-12
1 Sgt (SSgt)[1] (sqd ldr)
1 Cpl (Sgt)[1] (asst sqd leader)
10 Pvts (1 auto rifleman,
1 asst auto rifleman,
1 ammo bearer,
7 riflemen)
1 BAR, 11 rifles
(3 with M7 or M7 series GL)

WPNS

1-34[3]

1-5
1 LT (plat cdr)
1 SSgt (TSgt)[1] (plat sgt)
4 Pvts (2 [1 T-5] drivers,
2 messengers)
2 jeeps w/trailers
1 .50-cal MG
3(0)[1] bazookas
2 rifles
4 carbines

0-17

0-2
1 Sgt (SSgt)[1] (sect ldr)
1 Pvt (messenger)
1 rifle
1 carbine

0-5
1 Cpl (squad ldr)
4 Pvts (1 gunner,
1 asst gunner,
2 ammo bearers)
1 60mm mortar
3 carbines
2 pistols

LMG

0-12

0-2
1 Sgt (SSgt)[1] (sect ldr)
1 Pvt (messenger)
1 rifle
1 carbine

LMG

0-5
1 Cpl (squad ldr)
4 Pvts (1 gunner,
1 asst gunner,
2 ammo bearers)
1 .30-cal LMG M1919A4
3 carbines
2 pistols

Notes
Source: TO&E 7-17, July 15, 1943 and
February 26, 1944 plus Change 1 (June 30, 1944)
1 Changes dated February 26, 1944.
2 Spare weapons added June 30, 1944.
3 One rifleman per rifle platoon was equipped with an M1903A4 or M1C sniper rifle).
Small-arms distribution:
Pistols: mortar and LMG gunners and assistant gunners only.
Carbines: all officers, the first sergeant, the communication sergeant, the bugler, the messengers in company headquarters, and all weapons platoon personnel except the drivers and the section and squad leaders.
BAR: all automatic riflemen.
M1 rifles: all other personnel.
Grenade launchers: M7 series launchers (36) issued to the communication sergeant, each platoon guide, the LMG and mortar section leaders, the assistant squad leader and two riflemen in each rifle squad and the two drivers. The bugler carries an M8 grenade launcher.

Each rifle company weapons platoon maintained three bazookas until a general redistribution of bazookas in February 1944. After this date, the number per rifle company increased from three to five. All went to the company headquarters as unassigned weapons. In June 1944, the AGF further increased the rifle company commander's pool of unassigned weapons by six BARs and six submachine guns.

The July 1943 rifle company also consolidated all of its "basic privates" in the company headquarters. Basic privates had only basic (no specialist) training and were in excess of the personnel requirements of their parent unit. They functioned as "live-in" replacements to immediately make good the attrition resulting from accidents, disease, and other strength-draining absences. There were far too few of them to replace battle losses. That was the function of combat replacements. The advantage of basic privates was that they were already part of the unit and had time to become familiar with it before having to replace a unit member. When not needed as replacements they performed miscellaneous duties not otherwise provided for in the table of organization.

The infantry battalion

As in 1942 (and earlier) the weapons company was the infantry battalion base of fire. Its fighting elements were two heavy machine gun (HMG) platoons and an 81mm mortar platoon, but the "no-men" removed most of the drivers and

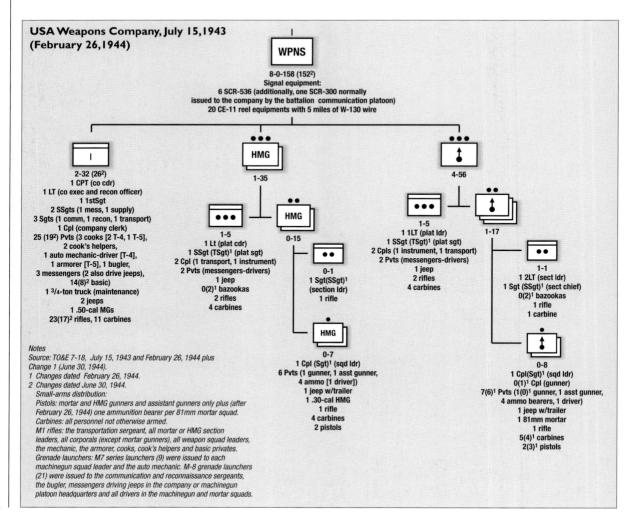

USA Weapons Company, July 15, 1943 (February 26, 1944)

WPNS

8-0-158 (152²)
Signal equipment:
6 SCR-536 (additionally, one SCR-300 normally issued to the company by the battalion communication platoon)
20 CE-11 reel equipments with 5 miles of W-130 wire

I

2-32 (26²)
1 CPT (co cdr)
1 LT (co exec and recon officer)
1 1stSgt
2 SSgts (1 mess, 1 supply)
3 Sgts (1 comm, 1 recon, 1 transport)
1 Cpl (company clerk)
25 (19²) Pvts (3 cooks [2 T-4, 1 T-5], 2 cook's helpers, 1 auto mechanic-driver [T-4], 1 armorer [T-5], 1 bugler, 3 messengers (2 also drive jeeps), 14(8)² basic)
1 ¾-ton truck (maintenance)
2 jeeps
1 .50-cal MGs
23(17)² rifles, 11 carbines

HMG
1-35

HMG
1-5
1 Lt (plat cdr)
1 SSgt (TSgt)¹ (plat sgt)
2 Cpl (1 transport, 1 instrument)
2 Pvts (messengers-drivers)
1 jeep
0(2)¹ bazookas
2 rifles
4 carbines

HMG
0-15

0-1
1 Sgt(SSgt)¹ (section ldr)
1 rifle

HMG
0-7
1 Cpl (Sgt)¹ (sqd ldr)
6 Pvts (1 gunner, 1 asst gunner, 4 ammo [1 driver])
1 jeep w/trailer
1 .30-cal HMG
1 rifle
4 carbines
2 pistols

4-56

1-5
1 1LT (plat ldr)
1 SSgt (TSgt)¹ (plat sgt)
2 Cpls (1 instrument, 1 transport)
2 Pvts (messengers-drivers)
1 jeep
2 rifles
4 carbines

1-17

1-1
1 2LT (sect ldr)
1 Sgt (SSgt)¹ (sect chief)
0(2)¹ bazookas
1 rifle
1 carbine

0-8
1 Cpl(Sgt)¹ (sqd ldr)
0(1)¹ Cpl (gunner)
7(6)¹ Pvts (1(0)¹ gunner, 1 asst gunner, 4 ammo bearers, 1 driver)
1 jeep w/trailer
1 81mm mortar
1 rifle
5(4)¹ carbines
2(3)¹ pistols

Notes
Source: TO&E 7-18, July 15, 1943 and February 26, 1944 plus Change 1 (June 30, 1944).
1 Changes dated February 26, 1944.
2 Changes dated June 30, 1944.
  Small-arms distribution:
Pistols: mortar and HMG gunners and assistant gunners only plus (after February 26, 1944) one ammunition bearer per 81mm mortar squad.
Carbines: all personnel not otherwise armed.
M1 rifles: the transportation sergeant, all mortar or HMG section leaders, all corporals (except mortar gunners), all weapon squad leaders, the mechanic, the armorer, cooks, cook's helpers and basic privates.
Grenade launchers: M7 series launchers (9) were issued to each machinegun squad leader and the auto mechanic. M-8 grenade launchers (21) were issued to the communication and reconnaissance sergeants, the bugler, messengers driving jeeps in the company or machinegun platoon headquarters and all drivers in the machinegun and mortar squads.

the platoon liaison agents (corporals) and assigned selected messengers and HMG ammunition bearers to drive most of the jeeps. To maintain the additional vehicles, the "no-men" added a company mechanic who drove a 3/4-ton truck that served as a maintenance vehicle. They also added a communication sergeant to the headquarters and placed a lieutenant in charge of each section in the 81mm mortar platoon. In February 1944, the "no-men" added a pair of bazookas to each mortar and HMG platoon.

The infantry battalion headquarters company also retained its 1942 configuration, but the "no-men" cut the number of vehicles from 21 to 14 and the number of drivers from 21 to six. In the communication platoon, wiremen and radio operators also had to double as drivers. The antitank platoon replaced its four squads of jeep-drawn 37mm M3 antitank guns with three larger squads with the new 1 1/2-ton, truck-drawn M1 57mm antitank gun. The M1 was an only slightly modified copy of the British "6-pounder" antitank gun. It was more powerful than the 37mm but more than three times as heavy. The fact that no high-explosive ammunition was produced for it put it at a disadvantage when engaging targets other than armored vehicles. Against the later German tanks it was less than adequate. The antitank platoon commander also had a .50-caliber machine gun for issue to one of his squads to mount on its 1 1/2-ton truck.

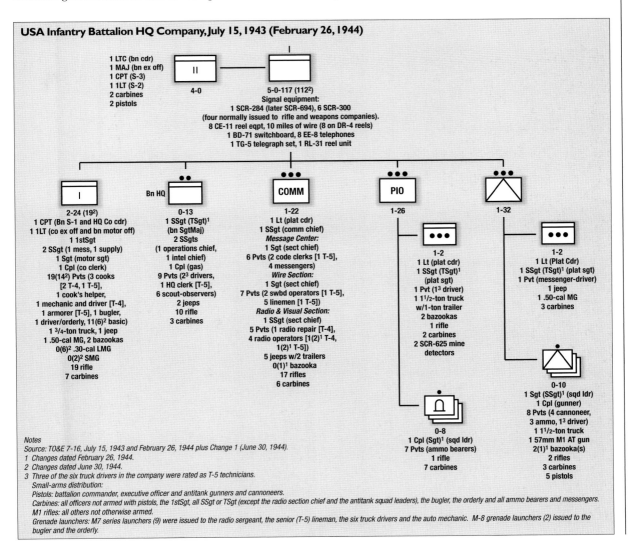

USA Infantry Battalion HQ Company, July 15, 1943 (February 26, 1944)

1 LTC (bn cdr)
1 MAJ (bn ex off)
1 CPT (S-3)
1 1LT (S-2)
2 carbines
2 pistols

4-0

5-0-117 (112²)
Signal equipment:
1 SCR-284 (later SCR-694), 6 SCR-300
(four normally issued to rifle and weapons companies).
8 CE-11 reel eqpt, 10 miles of wire (8 on DR-4 reels)
1 BD-71 switchboard, 8 EE-8 telephones
1 TG-5 telegraph set, 1 RL-31 reel unit

I — 2-24 (19²)
1 CPT (Bn S-1 and HQ Co cdr)
1 1LT (co ex off and bn motor off)
1 1stSgt
2 SSgts (1 mess, 1 supply)
1 Sgt (motor sgt)
1 Cpl (co clerk)
19(14²) Pvts (3 cooks
[2 T-4, 1 T-5],
1 cook's helper,
1 mechanic and driver [T-4],
1 armorer [T-5], 1 bugler,
1 driver/orderly, 11(6² basic)
1 ¾-ton truck, 1 jeep
1 .50-cal MG, 2 bazookas
0(6)² .30-cal LMG
0(2)² SMG
19 rifle
7 carbines

Bn HQ — 0-13
1 SSgt (TSgt)¹
(bn SgtMaj)
2 SSgts
(1 operations chief,
1 intel chief)
1 Cpl (gas)
9 Pvts (2³ drivers,
1 HQ clerk [T-5],
6 scout-observers)
2 jeeps
10 rifle
3 carbines

COMM — 1-22
1 Lt (plat cdr)
1 SSgt (comm chief)
Message Center:
1 Sgt (sect chief)
6 Pvts (2 code clerks [1 T-5],
4 messengers)
Wire Section:
1 Sgt (sect chief)
7 Pvts (2 swbd operators [1 T-5],
5 linemen [1 T-5])
Radio & Visual Section:
1 SSgt (sect chief)
5 Pvts (1 radio repair [T-4],
4 radio operators [1(2)¹ T-4,
1(2)¹ T-5])
5 jeeps w/2 trailers
0(1)¹ bazooka
17 rifles
6 carbines

PIO — 1-26

1-2
1 Lt (plat cdr)
1 SSgt (TSgt)¹
(plat sgt)
1 Pvt (1³ driver)
1 1½-ton truck
w/1-ton trailer
2 bazookas
1 rifle
2 carbines
2 SCR-625 mine
detectors

0-8
1 Cpl (Sgt)¹ (sqd ldr)
7 Pvts (ammo bearers)
1 rifle
7 carbines

1-32

1-2
1 Lt (Plat Cdr)
1 SSgt (TSgt)¹ plat sgt
1 Pvt (messenger-driver)
1 jeep
1 .50-cal MG
3 carbines

0-10
1 Sgt (SSgt)¹ (sqd ldr)
1 Cpl (gunner)
8 Pvts (4 cannoneer,
3 ammo, 1³ driver)
1 1½-ton truck
1 57mm M1 AT gun
2(1)¹ bazooka(s)
2 rifles
3 carbines
5 pistols

Notes
Source: TO&E 7-16, July 15, 1943 and February 26, 1944 plus Change 1 (June 30, 1944).
1 Changes dated February 26, 1944.
2 Changes dated June 30, 1944.
3 Three of the six truck drivers in the company were rated as T-5 technicians.
Small-arms distribution:
Pistols: battalion commander, executive officer and antitank gunners and cannoneers.
Carbines: all officers not armed with pistols, the 1stSgt, all SSgt or TSgt (except the radio section chief and the antitank squad leaders), the bugler, the orderly and all ammo bearers and messengers.
M1 rifles: all others not otherwise armed.
Grenade launchers: M7 series launchers (9) were issued to the radio sergeant, the senior (T-5) lineman, the six truck drivers and the auto mechanic. M-8 grenade launchers (2) issued to the bugler and the orderly.

13

The infantry regiment

Under the July 1943 reorganization the headquarters and service companies and the medical detachment of an infantry regiment were largely restored to what they had been in 1942. However, orderlies, cook's helpers, and others whose duties the "no-men" deemed nonessential or able to be combined with others (such as drivers acting as cook's helpers) were eliminated or cut back. Most company-sized units (other than the rifle companies) lost about 40 percent of their basic privates in February 1944.

The changes to the regimental antitank and cannon companies were much more significant. The antitank company would have three antitank platoons that were the same as those in the antitank platoons in the infantry battalions. It also retained its mine platoon, despite McNair's objection that it was a purely defensive unit and too specialized. The cannon company also survived, despite McNair's objection that there was little it could do that the division artillery (or cannon platoons in the headquarters company) could not. However, no regimental commander wanted to give up his own organic artillery. On the

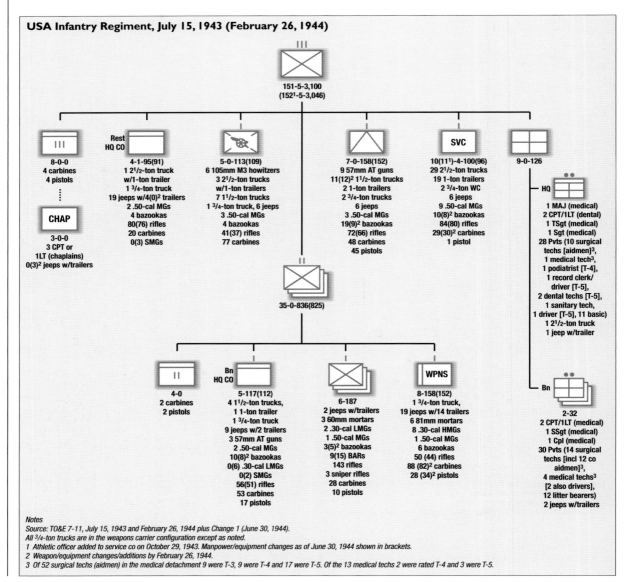

USA Infantry Regiment, July 15, 1943 (February 26, 1944)

Notes
Source: TO&E 7-11, July 15, 1943 and February 26, 1944 plus Change 1 (June 30, 1944).
All ³/₄-ton trucks are in the weapons carrier configuration except as noted.
1 Athletic officer added to service co on October 29, 1943. Manpower/equipment changes as of June 30, 1944 shown in brackets.
2 Weapon/equipment changes/additions by February 26, 1944.
3 Of 52 surgical techs (aidmen) in the medical detachment 9 were T-3, 9 were T-4 and 17 were T-5. Of the 13 medical techs 2 were rated T-4 and 3 were T-5.

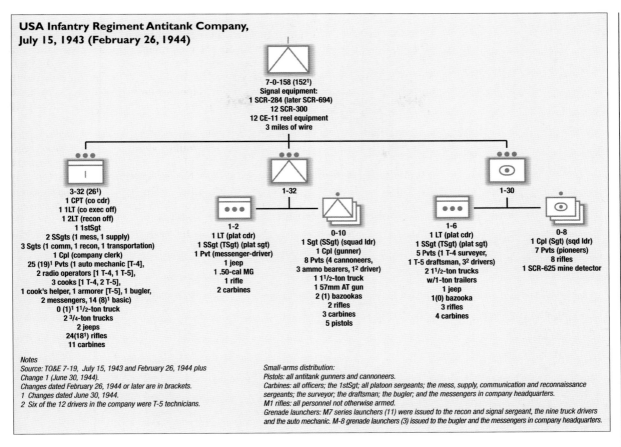

USA Infantry Regiment Antitank Company, July 15, 1943 (February 26, 1944)

7-0-158 (152[1])
Signal equipment:
1 SCR-284 (later SCR-694)
12 SCR-300
12 CE-11 reel equipment
3 miles of wire

3-32 (26[1])
1 CPT (co cdr)
1 1LT (co exec off)
1 2LT (recon off)
1 1stSgt
2 SSgts (1 mess, 1 supply)
3 Sgts (1 comm, 1 recon, 1 transportation)
1 Cpl (company clerk)
25 (19)[1] Pvts (1 auto mechanic [T-4],
2 radio operators [1 T-4, 1 T-5],
3 cooks [1 T-4, 2 T-5],
1 cook's helper, 1 armorer [T-5], 1 bugler,
2 messengers, 14 (8)[1] basic)
0 (1)[1] 1 1/2-ton truck
2 3/4-ton trucks
2 jeeps
24(18[1]) rifles
11 carbines

1-32

1-2
1 LT (plat cdr)
1 SSgt (TSgt) (plat sgt)
1 Pvt (messenger-driver)
1 jeep
1 .50-cal MG
1 rifle
2 carbines

0-10
1 Sgt (SSgt) (squad ldr)
1 Cpl (gunner)
8 Pvts (4 cannoneers,
3 ammo bearers, 1[2] driver)
1 1 1/2-ton truck
1 57mm AT gun
2 (1) bazookas
2 rifles
3 carbines
5 pistols

1-30

1-6
1 LT (plat cdr)
1 SSgt (TSgt) (plat sgt)
5 Pvts (1 T-4 surveyer,
1 T-5 draftsman, 3[2] drivers)
2 1 1/2-ton trucks
w/1-ton trailers
1 jeep
1(0) bazooka
3 rifles
4 carbines

0-8
1 Cpl (Sgt) (sqd ldr)
7 Pvts (pioneers)
8 rifles
1 SCR-625 mine detector

Notes
Source: TO&E 7-19, July 15, 1943 and February 26, 1944 plus
Change 1 (June 30, 1944).
Changes dated February 26, 1944 or later are in brackets.
1 Changes dated June 30, 1944.
2 Six of the 12 drivers in the company were T-5 technicians.

Small-arms distribution:
Pistols: all antitank gunners and cannoneers.
Carbines: all officers; the 1stSgt; all platoon sergeants; the mess, supply, communication and reconnaissance
sergeants; the surveyor; the draftsman; the bugler; and the messengers in company headquarters.
M1 rifles: all personnel not otherwise armed.
Grenade launchers: M7 series launchers (11) were issued to the recon and signal sergeant, the nine truck drivers
and the auto mechanic. M-8 grenade launchers (3) issued to the bugler and the messengers in company headquarters.

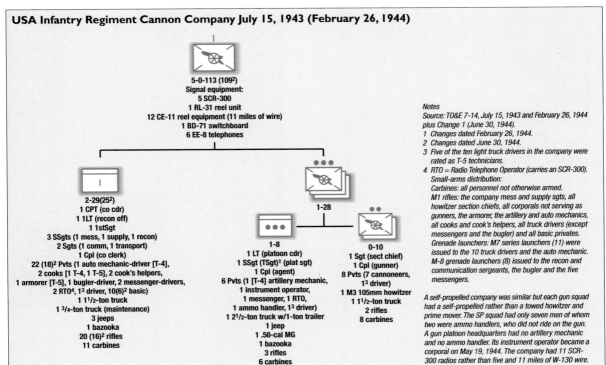

USA Infantry Regiment Cannon Company July 15, 1943 (February 26, 1944)

5-0-113 (109[2])
Signal equipment:
5 SCR-300
1 RL-31 reel unit
12 CE-11 reel equipment (11 miles of wire)
1 BD-71 switchboard
6 EE-8 telephones

2-29(25[2])
1 CPT (co cdr)
1 1LT (recon off)
1 1stSgt
3 SSgts (1 mess, 1 supply, 1 recon)
2 Sgts (1 comm, 1 transport)
1 Cpl (co clerk)
22 (18)[2] Pvts (1 auto mechanic-driver [T-4],
2 cooks [1 T-4, 1 T-5], 2 cook's helpers,
1 armorer [T-5], 1 bugler-driver, 2 messenger-drivers,
2 RTO[4], 1[3] driver, 10(6)[2] basic)
1 1 1/2-ton truck
1 3/4-ton truck (maintenance)
3 jeeps
1 bazooka
20 (16)[2] rifles
11 carbines

1-28

1-8
1 LT (platoon cdr)
1 SSgt (TSgt)[1] (plat sgt)
1 Cpl (agent)
6 Pvts (1 [T-4] artillery mechanic,
1 instrument operator,
1 messenger, 1 RTO,
1 ammo handler, 1[3] driver)
1 2 1/2-ton truck w/1-ton trailer
1 jeep
1 .50-cal MG
1 bazooka
3 rifles
6 carbines

0-10
1 Sgt (sect chief)
1 Cpl (gunner)
8 Pvts (7 cannoneers,
1[3] driver)
1 M3 105mm howitzer
1 1 1/2-ton truck
2 rifles
8 carbines

Notes
Source: TO&E 7-14, July 15, 1943 and February 26, 1944
plus Change 1 (June 30, 1944).
1 Changes dated February 26, 1944.
2 Changes dated June 30, 1944.
3 Five of the ten light truck drivers in the company were
rated as T-5 technicians.
4 RTO = Radio Telephone Operator (carries an SCR-300).
Small-arms distribution:
Carbines: all personnel not otherwise armed.
M1 rifles: the company mess and supply sgts, all
howitzer section chiefs, all corporals not serving as
gunners, the armorer, the artillery and auto mechanics,
all cooks and cook's helpers, all truck drivers (except
messengers and the bugler) and all basic privates.
Grenade launchers: M7 series launchers (11) were
issued to the 10 truck drivers and the auto mechanic.
M-8 grenade launchers (8) issued to the recon and
communication sergeants, the bugler and the five
messengers.

A self-propelled company was similar but each gun squad
had a self-propelled rather than a towed howitzer and
prime mover. The SP squad had only seven men of whom
two were ammo handlers, who did not ride on the gun.
A gun platoon headquarters had no artillery mechanic
and no ammo handler. Its instrument operator became a
corporal on May 19, 1944. The company had 11 SCR-
300 radios rather than five and 11 miles of W-130 wire.

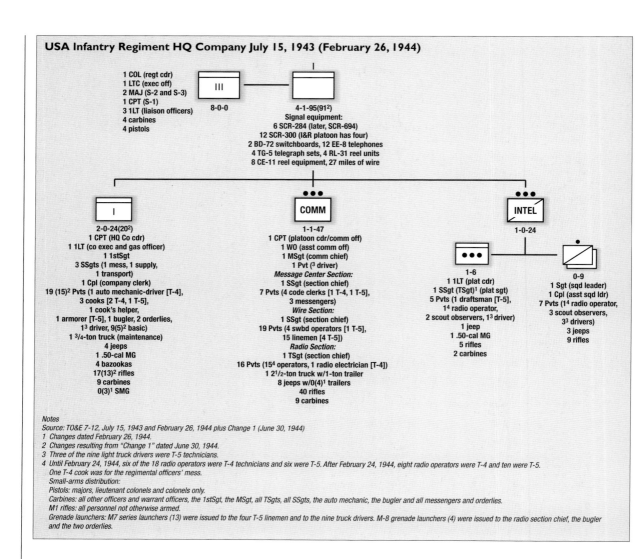

USA Infantry Regiment HQ Company July 15, 1943 (February 26, 1944)

III — 8-0-0
1 COL (regt cdr)
1 LTC (exec off)
2 MAJ (S-2 and S-3)
1 CPT (S-1)
3 1LT (liaison officers)
4 carbines
4 pistols

I — 4-1-95(91[2])
Signal equipment:
6 SCR-284 (later, SCR-694)
12 SCR-300 (I&R platoon has four)
2 BD-72 switchboards, 12 EE-8 telephones
4 TG-5 telegraph sets, 4 RL-31 reel units
8 CE-11 reel equipment, 27 miles of wire

I — 2-0-24(20[2])
1 CPT (HQ Co cdr)
1 1LT (co exec and gas officer)
1 1stSgt
3 SSgts (1 mess, 1 supply, 1 transport)
1 Cpl (company clerk)
19 (15)[2] Pvts (1 auto mechanic-driver [T-4],
3 cooks [2 T-4, 1 T-5],
1 cook's helper,
1 armorer [T-5], 1 bugler, 2 orderlies,
1[3] driver, 9(5)[2] basic)
1 3/4-ton truck (maintenance)
4 jeeps
1 .50-cal MG
4 bazookas
17(13)[2] rifles
9 carbines
0(3)[1] SMG

COMM — 1-1-47
1 CPT (platoon cdr/comm off)
1 WO (asst comm off)
1 MSgt (comm chief)
1 Pvt (3 driver)
Message Center Section:
1 SSgt (section chief)
7 Pvts (4 code clerks [1 T-4, 1 T-5],
3 messengers)
Wire Section:
1 SSgt (section chief)
19 Pvts (4 swbd operators [1 T-5],
15 linemen [4 T-5])
Radio Section:
1 TSgt (section chief)
16 Pvts (15[4] operators, 1 radio electrician [T-4])
1 2 1/2-ton truck w/1-ton trailer
8 jeeps w/0(4)[1] trailers
40 rifles
9 carbines

INTEL — 1-0-24

1-6
1 1LT (plat cdr)
1 SSgt (TSgt)[1] (plat sgt)
5 Pvts (1 draftsman [T-5],
1[4] radio operator,
2 scout observers, 1[3] driver)
1 jeep
1 .50-cal MG
5 rifles
2 carbines

0-9
1 Sgt (sqd leader)
1 Cpl (asst sqd ldr)
7 Pvts (1[4] radio operator,
3 scout observers,
3[3] drivers)
3 jeeps
9 rifles

Notes
Source: TO&E 7-12, July 15, 1943 and February 26, 1944 plus Change 1 (June 30, 1944)
1 Changes dated February 26, 1944.
2 Changes resulting from "Change 1" dated June 30, 1944.
3 Three of the nine light truck drivers were T-5 technicians.
4 Until February 24, 1944, six of the 18 radio operators were T-4 technicians and six were T-5. After February 24, 1944, eight radio operators were T-4 and ten were T-5.
One T-4 cook was for the regimental officers' mess.
Small-arms distribution:
Pistols: majors, lieutenant colonels and colonels only.
Carbines: all other officers and warrant officers, the 1stSgt, the MSgt, all TSgts, all SSgts, the auto mechanic, the bugler and all messengers and orderlies.
M1 rifles: all personnel not otherwise armed.
Grenade launchers: M7 series launchers (13) were issued to the four T-5 linemen and to the nine truck drivers. M-8 grenade launchers (4) were issued to the radio section chief, the bugler and the two orderlies.

On February 8, 1945 near Borgo di Bisano, Italy the II Corps artillery commander, Brigadier General Henry D. Jay, personally fires an M1 155mm howitzer belonging to Battery B, 936th Field Artillery Battalion. This was the 125,000th round to be fired by this unit. First standardized in May 1941 the M1 howitzer weighed 11,966 lb. in action and could loft its 95 lb. M107 high-explosive projectiles out to 16,355 yards, up to three times per minute. The M107 projectile had a broader rotating band than the M102 fired by the older M1918 howitzer. The M1918 could fire M107 projectiles only in a dire emergency and the M1 could not fire M102 projectiles at all. Both howitzers also used their own smoke and white phosphorus projectiles.

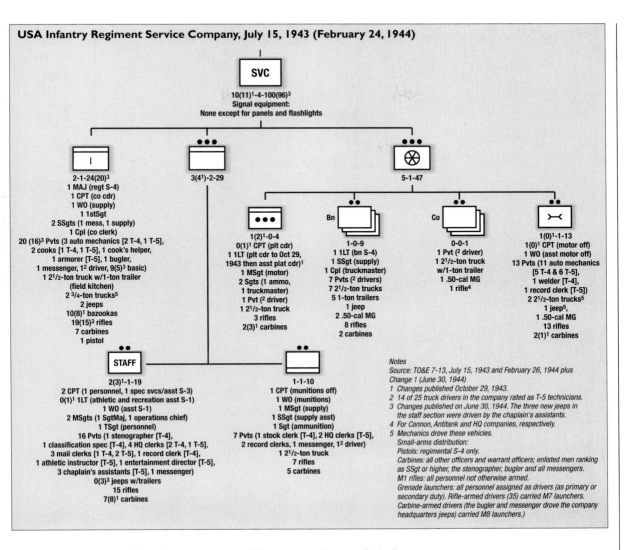

USA Infantry Regiment Service Company, July 15, 1943 (February 24, 1944)

SVC

10(11)[1]-4-100(96)[3]
Signal equipment:
None except for panels and flashlights

I

2-1-24(20)[3]
1 MAJ (regt S-4)
1 CPT (co cdr)
1 WO (supply)
1 1stSgt
2 SSgts (1 mess, 1 supply)
1 Cpl (co clerk)
20 (16)[3] Pvts (3 auto mechanics [2 T-4, 1 T-5],
2 cooks [1 T-4, 1 T-5], 1 cook's helper,
1 armorer [T-5], 1 bugler,
1 messenger, 1[2] driver, 9(5)[3] basic)
1 2¹/₂-ton truck w/1-ton trailer
(field kitchen)
2 ³/₄-ton trucks[5]
2 jeeps
10(8)[1] bazookas
19(15)[3] rifles
7 carbines
1 pistol

3(4[1])-2-29

1(2)[1]-0-4
0(1)[1] CPT (plt cdr)
1 1LT (plt cdr to Oct 29,
1943 then asst plat cdr)[1]
1 MSgt (motor)
2 Sgts (1 ammo,
1 truckmaster)
1 Pvt ([2] driver)
1 2¹/₂-ton truck
3 rifles
2(3)[1] carbines

Bn

1-0-9
1 1LT (bn S-4)
1 SSgt (supply)
1 Cpl (truckmaster)
7 Pvts ([2] drivers)
7 2¹/₂-ton trucks
5 1-ton trailers
1 jeep
2 .50-cal MG
8 rifles
2 carbines

5-1-47

Co

0-0-1
1 Pvt ([2] driver)
1 2¹/₂-ton truck
w/1-ton trailer
1 .50-cal MG
1 rifle[4]

1(0)[1]-1-13
1(0)[1] CPT (motor off)
1 WO (asst motor off)
13 Pvts (11 auto mechanics
[5 T-4 & 6 T-5],
1 welder [T-4],
1 record clerk [T-5])
2 2¹/₂-ton trucks[5]
1 jeep[5],
1 .50-cal MG
13 rifles
2(1)[1] carbines

STAFF

2(3)[1]-1-19
2 CPT (1 personnel, 1 spec svcs/asst S-3)
0(1)[1] 1LT (athletic and recreation asst S-1)
1 WO (asst S-1)
2 MSgts (1 SgtMaj, 1 operations chief)
1 TSgt (personnel)
16 Pvts (1 stenographer [T-4],
1 classification spec [T-4], 4 HQ clerks [2 T-4, 1 T-5],
3 mail clerks [1 T-4, 2 T-5], 1 record clerk [T-4],
1 athletic instructor [T-5], 1 entertainment director [T-5],
3 chaplain's assistants [T-5], 1 messenger)
0(3)[3] jeeps w/trailers
15 rifles
7(8)[1] carbines

1-1-10
1 CPT (munitions off)
1 WO (munitions)
1 MSgt (supply)
1 SSgt (supply asst)
1 Sgt (ammunition)
7 Pvts (1 stock clerk [T-4], 2 HQ clerks [T-5],
2 record clerks, 1 messenger, 1[2] driver)
1 2¹/₂-ton truck
7 rifles
5 carbines

Notes
Source: TO&E 7-13, July 15, 1943 and February 26, 1944 plus
Change 1 (June 30, 1944).
1 Changes published October 29, 1943.
2 14 of 25 truck drivers in the company rated as T-5 technicians.
3 Changes published on June 30, 1944. The three new jeeps in
the staff section were driven by the chaplain's assistants.
4 For Cannon, Antitank and HQ companies, respectively.
5 Mechanics drove these vehicles.
Small-arms distribution:
Pistols: regimental S-4 only.
Carbines: all other officers and warrant officers; enlisted men ranking
as SSgt or higher, the stenographer, bugler and all messengers.
M1 rifles: all personnel not otherwise armed.
Grenade launchers: all personnel assigned as drivers (as primary or
secondary duty). Rifle-armed drivers (35) carried M7 launchers.
Carbine-armed drivers (the bugler and messenger drove the company
headquarters jeeps) carried M8 launchers.)

other hand, the combat theaters were willing to exchange their heavy, maintenance-intensive, self-propelled guns for M3 towed howitzers.

In combat, infantry cannon companies used their M3 howitzers with their conspicuous and vulnerable 1½-ton prime movers to provide indirect fire support (within their range limits) to their parent regiments in much the same way as the 81mm mortars did for their respective battalions.

As it happened, however, not all regimental cannon companies switched to the M3. A few continued to use self-propelled weapons and the AGF later issued an official table of organization for them. These companies were supposed to have the same M7 self-propelled howitzer used by the armored divisions' artillery but the 81st Infantry Division cannon companies used T-12 half-track mounted 75mm guns in the Palaus and other weapons like the T-19 105mm self-propelled howitzer were probably used as well.

The division artillery

As per the infantry regiments, the "no-men" ruthlessly scrubbed the division artillery of nonessential personnel, saving over 100 men per battalion without reducing either firepower or the number of 2¹/₂-ton or 4-ton trucks. Nearly half the manpower saving came from the elimination of the battalion antitank platoons.

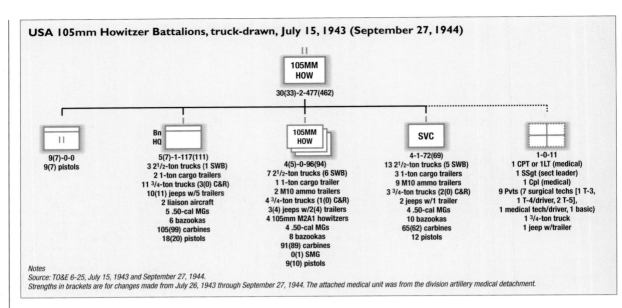

USA 105mm Howitzer Battalions, truck-drawn, July 15, 1943 (September 27, 1944)

105MM HOW
30(33)-2-477(462)

[Battalion, II]
9(7)-0-0
9(7) pistols

Bn HQ
5(7)-1-117(111)
3 2½-ton trucks (1 SWB)
2 1-ton cargo trailers
11 ¾-ton trucks (3(0) C&R)
10(11) jeeps w/5 trailers
2 liaison aircraft
5 .50-cal MGs
6 bazookas
105(99) carbines
18(20) pistols

105MM HOW
4(5)-0-96(94)
7 2½-ton trucks (6 SWB)
1 1-ton cargo trailer
2 M10 ammo trailers
4 ¾-ton trucks (1(0) C&R)
3(4) jeeps w/2(4) trailers
4 105mm M2A1 howitzers
4 .50-cal MGs
8 bazookas
91(89) carbines
0(1) SMG
9(10) pistols

SVC
4-1-72(69)
13 2½-ton trucks (5 SWB)
3 1-ton cargo trailers
9 M10 ammo trailers
3 ¾-ton trucks (2(0) C&R)
2 jeeps w/1 trailer
4 .50-cal MGs
10 bazookas
65(62) carbines
12 pistols

[medical]
1-0-11
1 CPT or 1LT (medical)
1 SSgt (sect leader)
1 Cpl (medical)
9 Pvts (7 surgical techs [1 T-3,
1 T-4/driver, 2 T-5],
1 medical tech/driver, 1 basic)
1 ¾-ton truck
1 jeep w/trailer

Notes
Source: TO&E 6-25, July 15, 1943 and September 27, 1944.
Strengths in brackets are for changes made from July 26, 1943 through September 27, 1944. The attached medical unit was from the division artillery medical detachment.

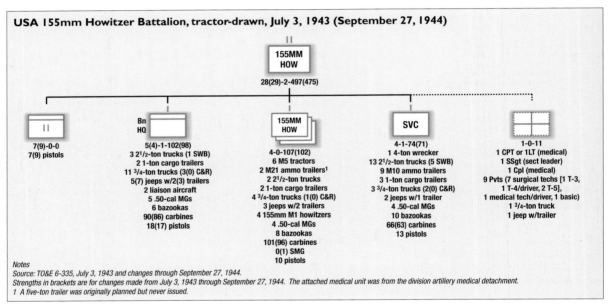

USA 155mm Howitzer Battalion, tractor-drawn, July 3, 1943 (September 27, 1944)

155MM HOW
28(29)-2-497(475)

[Battalion, II]
7(9)-0-0
7(9) pistols

Bn HQ
5(4)-1-102(98)
3 2½-ton trucks (1 SWB)
2 1-ton cargo trailers
11 ¾-ton trucks (3(0) C&R)
5(7) jeeps w/2(3) trailers
2 liaison aircraft
5 .50-cal MGs
6 bazookas
90(86) carbines
18(17) pistols

155MM HOW
4-0-107(102)
6 M5 tractors
2 M21 ammo trailers[1]
2 2½-ton trucks
2 1-ton cargo trailers
4 ¾-ton trucks (1(0) C&R)
3 jeeps w/2 trailers
4 155mm M1 howitzers
4 .50-cal MGs
8 bazookas
101(96) carbines
0(1) SMG
10 pistols

SVC
4-1-74(71)
1 4-ton wrecker
13 2½-ton trucks (5 SWB)
9 M10 ammo trailers
3 1-ton cargo trailers
3 ¾-ton trucks (2(0) C&R)
2 jeeps w/1 trailer
4 .50-cal MGs
10 bazookas
66(63) carbines
13 pistols

[medical]
1-0-11
1 CPT or 1LT (medical)
1 SSgt (sect leader)
1 Cpl (medical)
9 Pvts (7 surgical techs [1 T-3,
1 T-4/driver, 2 T-5],
1 medical tech/driver, 1 basic)
1 ¾-ton truck
1 jeep w/trailer

Notes
Source: TO&E 6-335, July 3, 1943 and changes through September 27, 1944.
Strengths in brackets are for changes made from July 3, 1943 through September 27, 1944. The attached medical unit was from the division artillery medical detachment.
1 A five-ton trailer was originally planned but never issued.

Of more significance was the introduction of the M5 high-speed artillery tractor. The first example of these left the assembly line in May 1943. Based on an unarmored M5 light tank chassis the M5 had plenty of power but only limited passenger and cargo space. Although it outperformed trucks off the roads, like most tracked vehicles it was slower and heavier, needed a lot more maintenance, and used a lot more fuel. However, the new M1 155mm howitzer was a heavy load for a 4-ton truck. In the European Theater, the M5 tractor was considered to be the superior prime mover for the 155mm howitzer but not for the 105mm. Nearly all 155mm howitzer battalions converted from trucks to tractors before the end of the war. In the Pacific Theater, where roads were few and soft sand or mud common but where distances were short, the tractors made more sense for 105mm howitzers. Therefore the 105mm howitzer battalions of 13 of the 19 infantry divisions sent to the Pacific Theater used tractors.

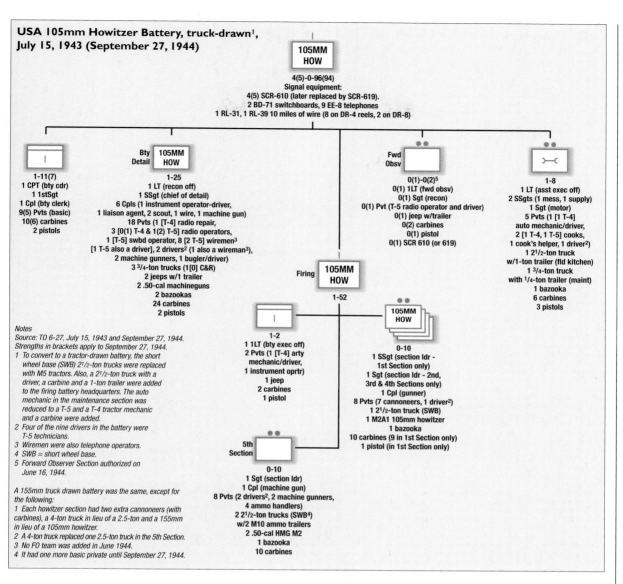

USA 105mm Howitzer Battery, truck-drawn[1], July 15, 1943 (September 27, 1944)

105MM HOW

4(5)-0-96(94)
Signal equipment:
4(5) SCR-610 (later replaced by SCR-619).
2 BD-71 switchboards, 9 EE-8 telephones
1 RL-31, 1 RL-39 10 miles of wire (8 on DR-4 reels, 2 on DR-8)

I

1-11(7)
1 CPT (bty cdr)
1 1stSgt
1 Cpl (bty clerk)
9(5) Pvts (basic)
10(6) carbines
2 pistols

Bty Detail — 105MM HOW

1-25
1 LT (recon off)
1 SSgt (chief of detail)
6 Cpls (1 instrument operator-driver,
1 liaison agent, 2 scout, 1 wire, 1 machine gun)
18 Pvts (1 [T-4] radio repair,
3 [0(1) T-4 & 1(2) T-5] radio operators,
1 [T-5] swbd operator, 8 [2 T-5] wiremen[3]
[1 T-5 also a driver], 2 drivers[2] (1 also a wireman[3]),
2 machine gunners, 1 bugler/driver)
3 ¾-ton trucks (1[0] C&R)
2 jeeps w/1 trailer
2 .50-cal machineguns
2 bazookas
24 carbines
2 pistols

Fwd Obsv

0(1)-0-0(2)[5]
0(1) 1LT (fwd obsv)
0(1) Sgt (recon)
0(1) Pvt (T-5 radio operator and driver)
0(1) jeep w/trailer
0(2) carbines
0(1) pistol
0(1) SCR 610 (or 619)

⊢⊣

1-8
1 LT (asst exec off)
2 SSgts (1 mess, 1 supply)
1 Sgt (motor)
5 Pvts (1 [1 T-4]
auto mechanic/driver,
2 [1 T-4, 1 T-5] cooks,
1 cook's helper, 1 driver[2])
1 2½-ton truck
w/1-ton trailer (fld kitchen)
1 ¾-ton truck
with ¼-ton trailer (maint)
1 bazooka
6 carbines
3 pistols

Firing — 105MM HOW

1-52

I

1-2
1 1LT (bty exec off)
2 Pvts (1 [T-4] arty
mechanic/driver,
1 instrument oprtr)
1 jeep
2 carbines
1 pistol

105MM HOW

0-10
1 SSgt (section ldr -
1st Section only)
1 Sgt (section ldr - 2nd,
3rd & 4th Sections only)
1 Cpl (gunner)
8 Pvts (7 cannoneers, 1 driver[2])
1 2½-ton truck (SWB)
1 M2A1 105mm howitzer
1 bazooka
10 carbines (9 in 1st Section only)
1 pistol (in 1st Section only)

5th Section

0-10
1 Sgt (section ldr)
1 Cpl (machine gun)
8 Pvts (2 drivers[2], 2 machine gunners,
4 ammo handlers)
2 2½-ton trucks (SWB[4])
w/2 M10 ammo trailers
2 .50-cal HMG M2
1 bazooka
10 carbines

Notes

Source: TO 6-27, July 15, 1943 and September 27, 1944.
Strengths in brackets apply to September 27, 1944.

1 *To convert to a tractor-drawn battery, the short wheel base (SWB) 2½-ton trucks were replaced with M5 tractors. Also, a 2½-ton truck with a driver, a carbine and a 1-ton trailer were added to the firing battery headquarters. The auto mechanic in the maintenance section was reduced to a T-5 and a T-4 tractor mechanic and a carbine were added.*
2 *Four of the nine drivers in the battery were T-5 technicians.*
3 *Wiremen were also telephone operators.*
4 *SWB = short wheel base.*
5 *Forward Observer Section authorized on June 16, 1944.*

A 155mm truck drawn battery was the same, except for the following:

1 *Each howitzer section had two extra cannoneers (with carbines), a 4-ton truck in lieu of a 2.5-ton and a 155mm in lieu of a 105mm howitzer.*
2 *A 4-ton truck replaced one 2.5-ton truck in the 5th Section.*
3 *No FO team was added in June 1944.*
4 *It had one more basic private until September 27, 1944.*

Unloading ammunition from an M5 tractor pulling two M10 ammunition trailers on Biak Island, New Guinea, June 8, 1944. The M5 was rated as a 13-ton tractor but because it was a tracked vehicle that figure referred to its weight, not its payload, which was only about 5,000 lb. It only had seats for nine men, including the driver but it could tow up to 20,000 lb.

USA 105mm Artillery Battalion Service Battery, truck-drawn, July 15, 1943 (September 27, 1944)

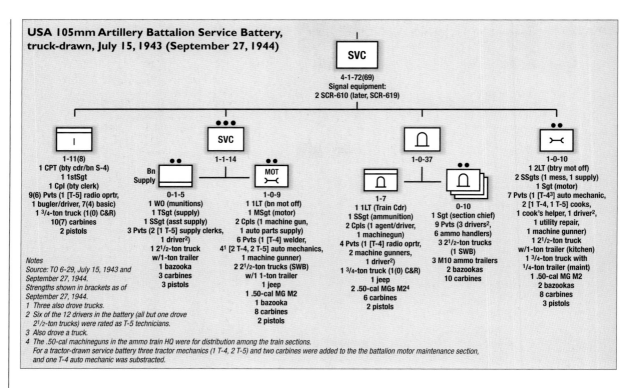

SVC

4-1-72(69)
Signal equipment:
2 SCR-610 (later, SCR-619)

I

1-11(8)
1 CPT (bty cdr/bn S-4)
1 1stSgt
1 Cpl (bty clerk)
9(6) Pvts (1 [T-5] radio oprtr,
1 bugler/driver, 7(4) basic)
1 3/4-ton truck (1(0) C&R)
10(7) carbines
2 pistols

SVC

1-1-14

Bn Supply

0-1-5
1 WO (munitions)
1 TSgt (supply)
1 SSgt (asst supply)
3 Pvts (2 [1 T-5] supply clerks,
1 driver[2])
1 21/2-ton truck
w/1-ton trailer
1 bazooka
3 carbines
3 pistols

MOT

1-0-9
1 1LT (bn mot off)
1 MSgt (motor)
2 Cpls (1 machine gun,
1 auto parts supply)
6 Pvts (1 [T-4] welder,
4[1] [2 T-4, 2 T-5] auto mechanics,
1 machine gunner)
2 21/2-ton trucks (SWB)
w/1 1-ton trailer
1 jeep
1 .50-cal MG M2
1 bazooka
8 carbines
2 pistols

(train symbol)

1-0-37

(train symbol)

1-7
1 1LT (Train Cdr)
1 SSgt (ammunition)
2 Cpls (1 agent/driver,
1 machinegun)
4 Pvts (1 [T-4] radio oprtr,
2 machine gunners,
1 driver[2])
1 3/4-ton truck (1(0) C&R)
1 jeep
2 .50-cal MGs M2[4]
6 carbines
2 pistols

(train symbol)

0-10
1 Sgt (section chief)
9 Pvts (3 drivers[2],
6 ammo handlers)
3 21/2-ton trucks
(1 SWB)
3 M10 ammo trailers
2 bazookas
10 carbines

(motor symbol)

1-0-10
1 2LT (btry mot off)
2 SSgts (1 mess, 1 supply)
1 Sgt (motor)
7 Pvts (1 [T-4[3]] auto mechanic,
2 [1 T-4, 1 T-5] cooks,
1 cook's helper, 1 driver[2],
1 utility repair,
1 machine gunner)
1 21/2-ton truck
w/1-ton trailer (kitchen)
1 3/4-ton truck with
1/4-ton trailer (maint)
1 .50-cal MG M2
2 bazookas
8 carbines
3 pistols

Notes
Source: TO 6-29, July 15, 1943 and September 27, 1944.
Strengths shown in brackets as of September 27, 1944.
1 Three also drove trucks.
2 Six of the 12 drivers in the battery (all but one drove 21/2-ton trucks) were rated as T-5 technicians.
3 Also drove a truck.
4 The .50-cal machineguns in the ammo train HQ were for distribution among the train sections.
For a tractor-drawn service battery three tractor mechanics (1 T-4, 2 T-5) and two carbines were added to the the battalion motor maintenance section, and one T-4 auto mechanic was substracted.

USA Infantry Division Artillery, July 15, 1943 (September 27, 1944)

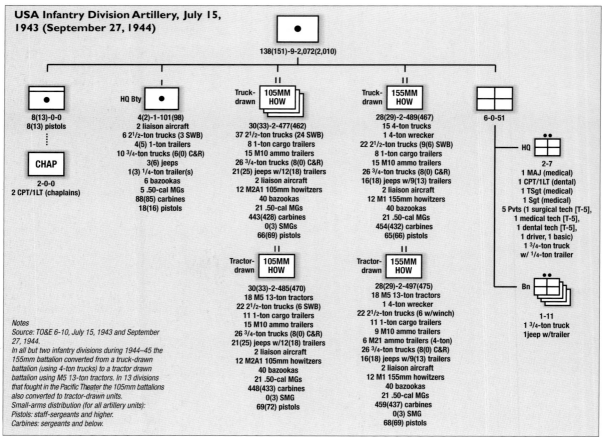

138(151)-9-2,072(2,010)

(dot symbol)

8(13)-0-0
8(13) pistols

CHAP

2-0-0
2 CPT/1LT (chaplains)

HQ Bty

4(2)-1-101(98)
2 liaison aircraft
6 21/2-ton trucks (3 SWB)
4(5) 1-ton trailers
10 3/4-ton trucks (6(0) C&R)
3(6) jeeps
1(3) 1/4-ton trailer(s)
6 bazookas
5 .50-cal MGs
88(85) carbines
18(16) pistols

Truck-drawn — 105MM HOW

30(33)-2-477(462)
37 21/2-ton trucks (24 SWB)
8 1-ton cargo trailers
15 M10 ammo trailers
26 3/4-ton trucks (8(0) C&R)
21(25) jeeps w/12(18) trailers
2 liaison aircraft
12 M2A1 105mm howitzers
40 bazookas
21 .50-cal MGs
443(428) carbines
0(3) SMGs
66(69) pistols

Tractor-drawn — 105MM HOW

30(33)-2-485(470)
18 M5 13-ton tractors
22 21/2-ton trucks (6 SWB)
11 1-ton cargo trailers
15 M10 ammo trailers
26 3/4-ton trucks (8(0) C&R)
21(25) jeeps w/12(18) trailers
2 liaison aircraft
12 M2A1 105mm howitzers
40 bazookas
21 .50-cal MGs
448(433) carbines
0(3) SMG
69(72) pistols

Truck-drawn — 155MM HOW

28(29)-2-489(467)
15 4-ton trucks
1 4-ton wrecker
22 21/2-ton trucks (9(6) SWB)
8 1-ton cargo trailers
15 M10 ammo trailers
26 3/4-ton trucks (8(0) C&R)
16(18) jeeps w/9(13) trailers
2 liaison aircraft
12 M1 155mm howitzers
40 bazookas
21 .50-cal MGs
454(432) carbines
65(66) pistols

Tractor-drawn — 155MM HOW

28(29)-2-497(475)
18 M5 13-ton tractors
1 4-ton wrecker
22 21/2-ton trucks (6 w/winch)
11 1-ton cargo trailers
9 M10 ammo trailers
6 M21 ammo trailers (4-ton)
26 3/4-ton trucks (8(0) C&R)
16(18) jeeps w/9(13) trailers
2 liaison aircraft
12 M1 155mm howitzers
40 bazookas
21 .50-cal MGs
459(437) carbines
0(3) SMG
68(69) pistols

(double box symbol)

6-0-51

HQ

2-7
1 MAJ (medical)
1 CPT/1LT (dental)
1 TSgt (medical)
1 Sgt (medical)
5 Pvts (1 surgical tech [T-5],
1 medical tech [T-5],
1 dental tech [T-5],
1 driver, 1 basic)
1 3/4-ton truck
w/ 1/4-ton trailer

Bn

1-11
1 3/4-ton truck
1jeep w/trailer

Notes
Source: TO&E 6-10, July 15, 1943 and September 27, 1944.
In all but two infantry divisions during 1944–45 the 155mm battalion converted from a truck-drawn battalion (using 4-ton trucks) to a tractor drawn battalion using M5 13-ton tractors. In 13 divisions that fought in the Pacific Theater the 105mm battalions also converted to tractor-drawn units.
Small-arms distribution (for all artillery units):
Pistols: staff-sergeants and higher.
Carbines: sergeants and below.

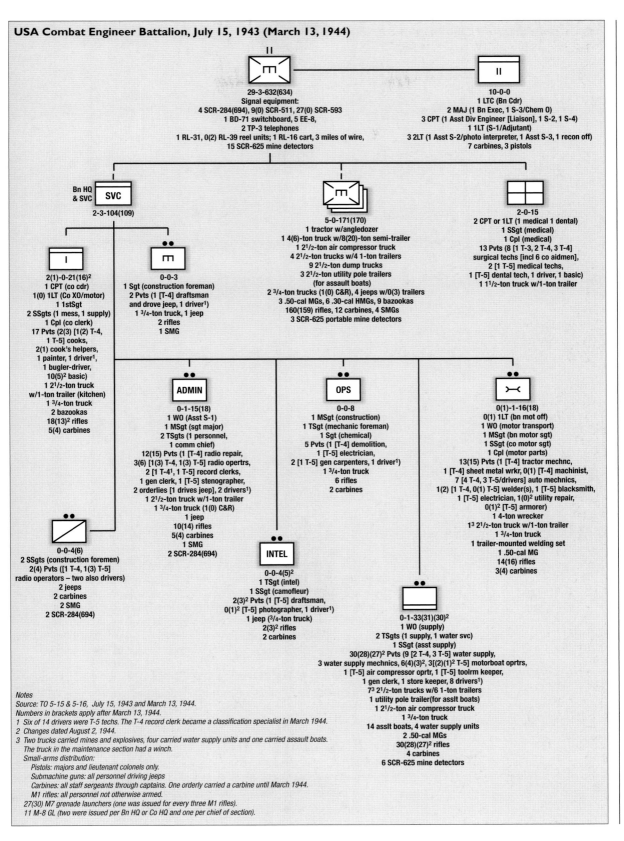

USA Combat Engineer Battalion, July 15, 1943 (March 13, 1944)

29-3-632(634)
Signal equipment:
4 SCR-284(694), 9(0) SCR-511, 27(0) SCR-593
1 BD-71 switchboard, 5 EE-8,
2 TP-3 telephones
1 RL-31, 0(2) RL-39 reel units; 1 RL-16 cart, 3 miles of wire,
15 SCR-625 mine detectors

10-0-0
1 LTC (Bn Cdr)
2 MAJ (1 Bn Exec, 1 S-3/Chem O)
3 CPT (1 Asst Div Engineer [Liaison], 1 S-2, 1 S-4)
1 1LT (S-1/Adjutant)
3 2LT (1 Asst S-2/photo interpreter, 1 Asst S-3, 1 recon off)
7 carbines, 3 pistols

Bn HQ & SVC — SVC
2-3-104(109)

5-0-171(170)
1 tractor w/angledozer
1 4(6)-ton truck w/8(20)-ton semi-trailer
1 2 1/2-ton air compressor truck
4 2 1/2-ton trucks w/4 1-ton trailers
9 2 1/2-ton dump trucks
3 2 1/2-ton utility pole trailers
(for assault boats)
2 3/4-ton trucks (1(0) C&R), 4 jeeps w/0(3) trailers
3 .50-cal MGs, 6 .30-cal HMGs, 9 bazookas
160(159) rifles, 12 carbines, 4 SMGs
3 SCR-625 portable mine detectors

2-0-15
2 CPT or 1LT (1 medical 1 dental)
1 SSgt (medical)
1 Cpl (medical)
13 Pvts (8 [1 T-3, 2 T-4, 3 T-4]
surgical techs [incl 6 co aidmen],
2 [1 T-5] medical techs,
1 [T-5] dental tech, 1 driver, 1 basic)
1 1 1/2-ton truck w/1-ton trailer

2(1)-0-21(16)[2]
1 CPT (co cdr)
1(0) 1LT (Co XO/motor)
1 1stSgt
2 SSgts (1 mess, 1 supply)
1 Cpl (co clerk)
17 Pvts (2(3) [1(2) T-4,
1 T-5] cooks,
2(1) cook's helpers,
1 painter, 1 driver[1],
1 bugler-driver,
10(5)[2] basic)
1 2 1/2-ton truck
w/1-ton trailer (kitchen)
1 3/4-ton truck
2 bazookas
18(13)[2] rifles
5(4) carbines

0-0-3
1 Sgt (construction foreman)
2 Pvts (1 [T-4] draftsman
and drove jeep, 1 driver[1])
1 3/4-ton truck, 1 jeep
2 rifles
1 SMG

ADMIN
0-1-15(18)
1 WO (Asst S-1)
1 MSgt (sgt major)
2 TSgts (1 personnel,
1 comm chief)
12(15) Pvts (1 [T-4] radio repair,
3(6) [1(3) T-4, 1(3) T-5] radio oprtrs,
2 [1 T-4[1], 1 T-5] record clerks,
1 gen clerk, 1 [T-5] stenographer,
2 orderlies [1 drives jeep, 2 drivers[1])
1 2 1/2-ton truck w/1-ton trailer
1 3/4-ton truck (1(0) C&R)
1 jeep
10(14) rifles
5(4) carbines
1 SMG
2 SCR-284(694)

OPS
0-0-8
1 MSgt (construction)
1 TSgt (mechanic foreman)
1 Sgt (chemical)
5 Pvts (1 [T-4] demolition,
1 [T-5] electrician,
2 [1 T-5] gen carpenters, 1 driver[1])
1 3/4-ton truck
6 rifles
2 carbines

0(1)-1-16(18)
0(1) 1LT (bn mot off)
1 WO (motor transport)
1 MSgt (bn motor sgt)
1 SSgt (co motor sgt)
1 Cpl (motor parts)
13(15) Pvts (1 [T-4] tractor mechnc,
1 [T-4] sheet metal wrkr, 0(1) [T-4] machinist,
7 [4 T-4, 3 T-5/drivers] auto mechnics,
1(2) [1 T-4, 0(1) T-5] welder(s), 1 [T-5] blacksmith,
1 [T-5] electrician, 1(0)[2] utility repair,
0(1)[2] [T-5] armorer)
1 4-ton wrecker
1[3] 2 1/2-ton truck w/1-ton trailer
1 3/4-ton truck
1 trailer-mounted welding set
1 .50-cal MG
14(16) rifles
3(4) carbines

0-0-4(6)
2 SSgts (construction foremen)
2(4) Pvts ([1 T-4, 1(3) T-5]
radio operators – two also drivers)
2 jeeps
2 carbines
2 SMG
2 SCR-284(694)

INTEL
0-0-4(5)[2]
1 TSgt (intel)
1 SSgt (camofleur)
2(3)[2] Pvts (1 [T-5] draftsman,
0(1)[2] [T-5] photographer, 1 driver[1])
1 jeep (3/4-ton truck)
2(3)[2] rifles
2 carbines

0-1-33(31)(30)[2]
1 WO (supply)
2 TSgts (1 supply, 1 water svc)
1 SSgt (asst supply)
30(28)(27)[2] Pvts (9 [2 T-4, 3 T-5] water supply,
3 water supply mechnics, 6(4)(3)[2], 3[(2)(1)[2] T-5] motorboat oprtrs,
1 [T-5] air compressor oprtr, 1 [T-5] toolrm keeper,
1 gen clerk, 1 store keeper, 8 drivers[1])
7[3] 2 1/2-ton trucks w/6 1-ton trailers
1 utility pole trailer(for asslt boats)
1 2 1/2-ton air compressor truck
1 3/4-ton truck
14 asslt boats, 4 water supply units
2 .50-cal MGs
30(28)(27)[2] rifles
4 carbines
6 SCR-625 mine detectors

Notes
Source: TO 5-15 & 5-16, July 15, 1943 and March 13, 1944.
Numbers in brackets apply after March 13, 1944.
1 Six of 14 drivers were T-5 techs. The T-4 record clerk became a classification specialist in March 1944.
2 Changes dated August 2, 1944.
3 Two trucks carried mines and explosives, four carried water supply units and one carried assault boats.
The truck in the maintenance section had a winch.
Small-arms distribution:
Pistols: majors and lieutenant colonels only.
Submachine guns: all personnel driving jeeps.
Carbines: all staff sergeants through captains. One orderly carried a carbine until March 1944.
M1 rifles: all personnel not otherwise armed.
27(30) M7 grenade launchers (one was issued for every three M1 rifles).
11 M-8 GL (two were issued per Bn HQ or Co HQ and one per chief of section).

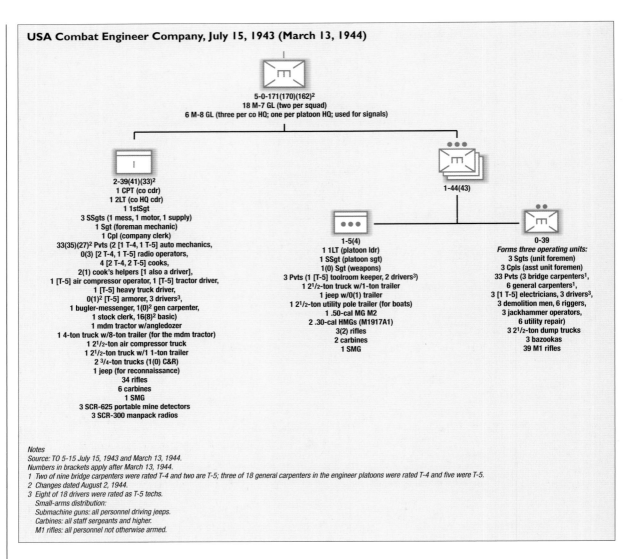

USA Combat Engineer Company, July 15, 1943 (March 13, 1944)

5-0-171(170)(162)[2]
18 M-7 GL (two per squad)
6 M-8 GL (three per co HQ; one per platoon HQ; used for signals)

2-39(41)(33)[2]
1 CPT (co cdr)
1 2LT (co HQ cdr)
1 1stSgt
3 SSgts (1 mess, 1 motor, 1 supply)
1 Sgt (foreman mechanic)
1 Cpl (company clerk)
33(35)(27)[2] Pvts (2 [1 T-4, 1 T-5] auto mechanics,
0(3) [2 T-4, 1 T-5] radio operators,
4 [2 T-4, 2 T-5] cooks,
2(1) cook's helpers [1 also a driver],
1 [T-5] air compressor operator, 1 [T-5] tractor driver,
1 [T-5] heavy truck driver,
0(1)[2] [T-5] armorer, 3 drivers[3],
1 bugler-messenger, 1(0)[2] gen carpenter,
1 stock clerk, 16(8)[2] basic)
1 mdm tractor w/angledozer
1 4-ton truck w/8-ton trailer (for the mdm tractor)
1 2½-ton air compressor truck
1 2½-ton truck w/1 1-ton trailer
2 ¾-ton trucks (1(0) C&R)
1 jeep (for reconnaissance)
34 rifles
6 carbines
1 SMG
3 SCR-625 portable mine detectors
3 SCR-300 manpack radios

1-44(43)

1-5(4)
1 1LT (platoon ldr)
1 SSgt (platoon sgt)
1(0) Sgt (weapons)
3 Pvts (1 [T-5] toolroom keeper, 2 drivers[3])
1 2½-ton truck w/1-ton trailer
1 jeep w/0(1) trailer
1 2½-ton utility pole trailer (for boats)
1 .50-cal MG M2
2 .30-cal HMGs (M1917A1)
3(2) rifles
2 carbines
1 SMG

0-39
Forms three operating units:
3 Sgts (unit foremen)
3 Cpls (asst unit foremen)
33 Pvts (3 bridge carpenters[1],
6 general carpenters[1],
3 [1 T-5] electricians, 3 drivers[3],
3 demolition men, 6 riggers,
3 jackhammer operators,
6 utility repair)
3 2½-ton dump trucks
3 bazookas
39 M1 rifles

Notes
Source: TO 5-15 July 15, 1943 and March 13, 1944.
Numbers in brackets apply after March 13, 1944.
1 Two of nine bridge carpenters were rated T-4 and two are T-5; three of 18 general carpenters in the engineer platoons were rated T-4 and five were T-5.
2 Changes dated August 2, 1944.
3 Eight of 18 drivers were rated as T-5 techs.
 Small-arms distribution:
 Submachine guns: all personnel driving jeeps.
 Carbines: all staff sergeants and higher.
 M1 rifles: all personnel not otherwise armed.

Apart from its substitution of tractors for trucks in the four gun sections and "fifth" (or ammunition) section in each howitzer battery, conversion from trucks to tractors required only the addition of a 2½-ton truck, trailer, and driver to each firing battery headquarters, the addition of a tractor mechanic to each howitzer battery maintenance section, and a net increase of two mechanics in the battalion maintenance section (service battery). The extra truck carried the personnel and ammunition, for which there was no space in the tractors.

The combat engineer battalion

From 1942 this battalion underwent serious "de-fatting" (as McNair called it), but its basic engineering capabilities survived the "no-men's" axe. Its combat capabilities remained strictly defensive.

Other divisional units

Like the division engineer battalion, the medical battalion and signal, ordnance, and quartermaster companies were trimmed mostly of nonessential personnel and vehicles. However, the medical battalion did lose some ambulances and stretcher teams from its collecting companies. The signal company lost its radio intelligence platoon (McNair felt that this was a function more appropriate for

USA Infantry Division Medical Battalion, July 15, 1943 (February 14, 1945)

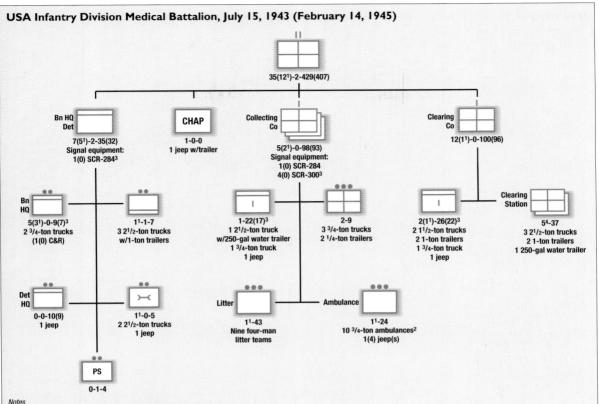

Notes

Source: TO 8-15, 8-16, 8-17 and 8-18 (July 15, 1943 and February 14, 1945).

Numbers in brackets apply after July 3, 1944.

1 Twelve of the battalion's 35 officers belonged to the Medical Administrative Corps. MAC officers supervised non-medical activities such as supply, administration and motor maintenance.

2 On September 13, 1943, 3/4-ton trucks equipped as ambulances were ordered to replace the original panel ambulances. The new ambulances did not arrive until very late in the war, however.

3 Battalion radio operator, repairman and radios deleted on September 3, 1943. The number of basic privates was reduced as of July 3, 1944.

4 Includes a dental officer.

USA Infantry Division Quartermaster Company, July 15, 1943 (February 19, 1944)

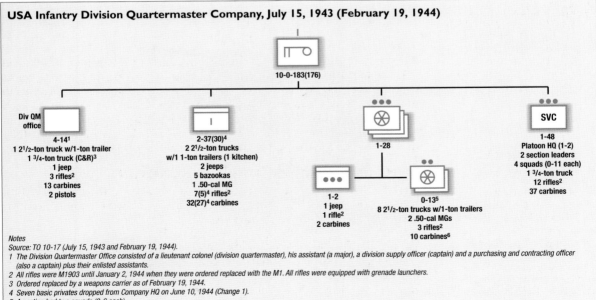

Notes

Source: TO 10-17 (July 15, 1943 and February 19, 1944).

1 The Division Quartermaster Office consisted of a lieutenant colonel (division quartermaster), his assistant (a major), a division supply officer (captain) and a purchasing and contracting officer (also a captain) plus their enlisted assistants.

2 All rifles were M1903 until January 2, 1944 when they were ordered replaced with the M1. All rifles were equipped with grenade launchers.

3 Ordered replaced by a weapons carrier as of February 19, 1944.

4 Seven basic privates dropped from Company HQ on June 10, 1944 (Change 1).

5 A section had two squads (0-6 each).

6 One M1 carbine out of 10 (or major fraction thereof) was equipped with an M8 grenade launcher.

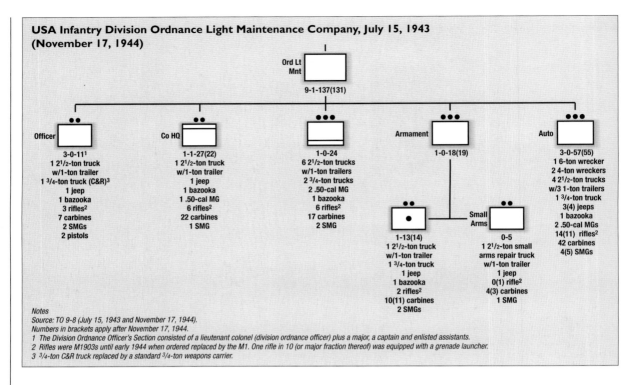

USA Infantry Division Ordnance Light Maintenance Company, July 15, 1943 (November 17, 1944)

Ord Lt Mnt

9-1-137(131)

Officer
3-0-11[1]
1 2½-ton truck
w/1-ton trailer
1 ¾-ton truck (C&R)[3]
1 jeep
1 bazooka
3 rifles[2]
7 carbines
2 SMGs
2 pistols

Co HQ
1-1-27(22)
1 2½-ton truck
w/1-ton trailer
1 jeep
1 bazooka
1 .50-cal MG
6 rifles[2]
22 carbines
1 SMG

1-0-24
6 2½-ton trucks
w/1-ton trailers
2 ¾-ton trucks
2 .50-cal MG
1 bazooka
6 rifles[2]
17 carbines
2 SMG

Armament
1-0-18(19)

1-13(14)
1 2½-ton truck
w/1-ton trailer
1 ¾-ton truck
1 jeep
1 bazooka
2 rifles[2]
10(11) carbines
2 SMGs

Small Arms
0-5
1 2½-ton small
arms repair truck
w/1-ton trailer
1 jeep
0(1) rifle[2]
4(3) carbines
1 SMG

Auto
3-0-57(55)
1 6-ton wrecker
2 4-ton wreckers
4 2½-ton trucks
w/3 1-ton trailers
1 ¾-ton truck
3(4) jeeps
1 bazooka
2 .50-cal MGs
14(11) rifles[2]
42 carbines
4(5) SMGs

Notes
Source: TO 9-8 (July 15, 1943 and November 17, 1944).
Numbers in brackets apply after November 17, 1944.
1 The Division Ordnance Officer's Section consisted of a lieutenant colonel (division ordnance officer) plus a major, a captain and enlisted assistants.
2 Rifles were M1903s until early 1944 when ordered replaced by the M1. One rifle in 10 (or major fraction thereof) was equipped with a grenade launcher.
3 ¾-ton C&R truck replaced by a standard ¾-ton weapons carrier.

higher headquarters). The new "special troops" headquarters administratively commanded the quartermaster (with service platoon intact), signal, ordnance, division headquarters company, and military police platoon.

The division reconnaissance troop was greatly simplified, its reconnaissance platoons operating separate armored car and jeep sections, but the number of personnel who could dismount and fight on foot remained small.

One of many M3 half-tracks camouflaged for the winter terrain near Thionville, France, pictured on January 12, 1944. This one carries a .50-cal machine gun. The only half-tracks organic to an infantry division at this time belonged to the reconnaissance troop, but they could also be found in supporting tank, antitank and antiaircraft artillery battalions.

24

USA Infantry Division Cavalry Recon Troop, July 15, 1943

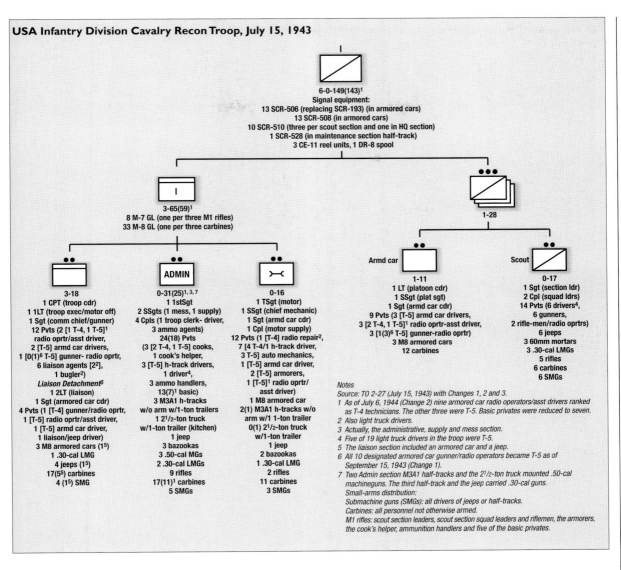

6-0-149(143)[1]
Signal equipment:
13 SCR-506 (replacing SCR-193) (in armored cars)
13 SCR-508 (in armored cars)
10 SCR-510 (three per scout section and one in HQ section)
1 SCR-528 (in maintenance section half-track)
3 CE-11 reel units, 1 DR-8 spool

3-65(59)[1]
8 M-7 GL (one per three M1 rifles)
33 M-8 GL (one per three carbines)

1-28

3-18
1 CPT (troop cdr)
1 1LT (troop exec/motor off)
1 Sgt (comm chief/gunner)
12 Pvts (2 [1 T-4, 1 T-5][1]
radio oprtr/asst driver,
2 [T-5] armd car drivers,
1 [0(1)[6] T-5] gunner- radio oprtr,
6 liaison agents [2[2]],
1 bugler[2])
Liaison Detachment[5]
1 2LT (liaison)
1 Sgt (armored car cdr)
4 Pvts (1 [T-4] gunner/radio oprtr,
1 [T-5] radio oprtr/asst driver,
1 [T-5] armd car driver,
1 liaison/jeep driver)
3 M8 armored cars (1[5])
1 .30-cal LMG
4 jeeps (1[5])
17(5[5]) carbines
4 (1[5]) SMG

ADMIN
0-31(25)[1, 3, 7]
1 1stSgt
2 SSgts (1 mess, 1 supply)
4 Cpls (1 troop clerk- driver,
3 ammo agents)
24(18) Pvts
(3 [2 T-4, 1 T-5] cooks,
1 cook's helper,
3 [T-5] h-track drivers,
1 driver[4],
3 ammo handlers,
13(7)[1] basic)
3 M3A1 h-tracks
w/o arm w/1-ton trailers
1 2½-ton truck
w/1-ton trailer (kitchen)
1 jeep
3 bazookas
3 .50-cal MGs
2 .30-cal LMGs
9 rifles
17(11)[1] carbines
5 SMGs

0-16
1 TSgt (motor)
1 SSgt (chief mechanic)
1 Sgt (armd car cdr)
1 Cpl (motor supply)
12 Pvts (1 [T-4] radio repair[2],
7 [4 T-4/1 h-track driver,
3 T-5] auto mechanics,
1 [T-5] armd car driver,
2 [T-5] armorers,
1 [T-5][1] radio oprtr/
asst driver)
1 M8 armored car
2(1) M3A1 h-tracks w/o
arm w/1 1-ton trailer
0(1) 2½-ton truck
w/1-ton trailer
1 jeep
2 bazookas
1 .30-cal LMG
2 rifles
11 carbines
3 SMGs

Armd car
1-11
1 LT (platoon cdr)
1 SSgt (plat sgt)
1 Sgt (armd car cdr)
9 Pvts (3 [T-5] armd car drivers,
3 [2 T-4, 1 T-5][1] radio oprtr-asst driver,
3 [1(3)[6] T-5] gunner-radio oprtr)
3 M8 armored cars
12 carbines

Scout
0-17
1 Sgt (section ldr)
2 Cpl (squad ldrs)
14 Pvts (6 drivers[4],
6 gunners,
2 rifle-men/radio oprtrs)
6 jeeps
3 60mm mortars
3 .30-cal LMGs
5 rifles
6 carbines
6 SMGs

Notes
Source: TO 2-27 (July 15, 1943) with Changes 1, 2 and 3.
1 *As of July 6, 1944 (Change 2) nine armored car radio operators/asst drivers ranked as T-4 technicians. The other three were T-5. Basic privates were reduced to seven.*
2 *Also light truck drivers.*
3 *Actually, the administrative, supply and mess section.*
4 *Five of 19 light truck drivers in the troop were T-5.*
5 *The liaison section included an armored car and a jeep.*
6 *All 10 designated armored car gunner/radio operators became T-5 as of September 15, 1943 (Change 1).*
7 *Two Admin section M3A1 half-tracks and the 2½-ton truck mounted .50-cal machineguns. The third half-track and the jeep carried .30-cal guns.*
Small-arms distribution:
Submachine guns (SMGs): all drivers of jeeps or half-tracks.
Carbines: all personnel not otherwise armed.
M1 rifles: scout section leaders, scout section squad leaders and riflemen, the armorers, the cook's helper, ammunition handlers and five of the basic privates.

Troops (probably from a battalion pioneer platoon) of the 407th Infantry, 102d Division, 9th US Army carry 10 lb. blocks of dynamite charges for destroying obstacles near the Roer River at Linnich, Germany, February 23, 1945.

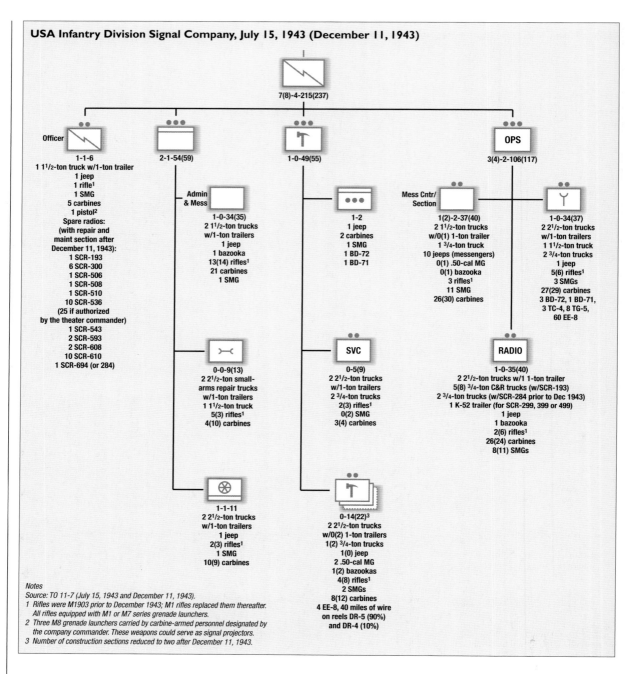

The division headquarters and headquarters company experienced only minor personnel economies after 1942, the defense platoon having narrowly escaped McNair's axe. Attached to the company was the division band (actually two separate bands) which provided music for ceremonies (and extra guards, laborers, etc.). This band replaced the former infantry and artillery regimental bands.

One unit that actually experienced an increase was the division military police platoon. Its five 11-man MP squads proved so inadequate that in September 1944 the War Department increased the platoon to eight squads and gave its platoon leader an executive officer to run the platoon while he focused on his primary role of division provost marshal.

USA Infantry Division HQ and HQ Company, July 15, 1943 (January 13, 1945)

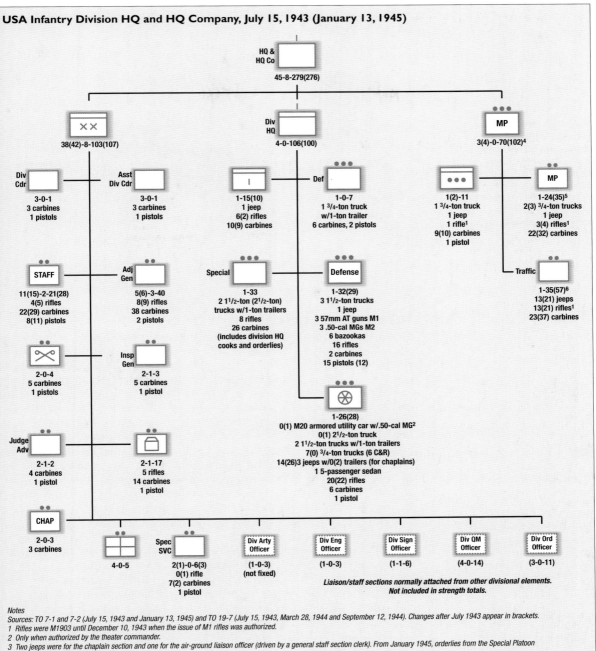

HQ & HQ Co
45-8-279(276)

XX
38(42)-8-103(107)

Div HQ
4-0-106(100)

MP
3(4)-0-70(102)[4]

Div Cdr
3-0-1
3 carbines
1 pistols

Asst Div Cdr
3-0-1
3 carbines
1 pistols

1-15(10)
1 jeep
6(2) rifles
10(9) carbines

Def
1-0-7
1 ³/₄-ton truck
w/1-ton trailer
6 carbines, 2 pistols

1(2)-11
1 ³/₄-ton truck
1 jeep
1 rifle[1]
9(10) carbines
1 pistol

MP
1-24(35)[5]
2(3) ³/₄-ton trucks
1 jeep
3(4) rifles[1]
22(32) carbines

STAFF
11(15)-2-21(28)
4(5) rifles
22(29) carbines
8(11) pistols

Adj Gen
5(6)-3-40
8(9) rifles
38 carbines
2 pistols

Special
1-33
2 1¹/₂-ton (2¹/₂-ton)
trucks w/1-ton trailers
8 rifles
26 carbines
(includes division HQ
cooks and orderlies)

Defense
1-32(29)
3 1¹/₂-ton trucks
1 jeep
3 57mm AT guns M1
3 .50-cal MGs M2
6 bazookas
16 rifles
2 carbines
15 pistols (12)

Traffic
1-35(57)[6]
13(21) jeeps
13(21) rifles[1]
23(37) carbines

2-0-4
5 carbines
1 pistols

Insp Gen
2-1-3
5 carbines
1 pistol

Judge Adv
2-1-2
4 carbines
1 pistol

2-1-17
5 rifles
14 carbines
1 pistol

1-26(28)
0(1) M20 armored utility car w/.50-cal MG[2]
0(1) 2¹/₂-ton truck
2 1¹/₂-ton trucks w/1-ton trailers
7(0) ³/₄-ton trucks (6 C&R)
14(26)3 jeeps w/0(2) trailers (for chaplains)
1 5-passenger sedan
20(22) rifles
6 carbines
1 pistol

CHAP
2-0-3
3 carbines

4-0-5

Spec SVC
2(1)-0-6(3)
0(1) rifle
7(2) carbines
1 pistol

Div Arty Officer
(1-0-3)
(not fixed)

Div Eng Officer
(1-0-3)

Div Sign Officer
(1-1-6)

Div QM Officer
(4-0-14)

Div Ord Officer
(3-0-11)

*Liaison/staff sections normally attached from other divisional elements.
Not included in strength totals.*

Notes
Sources: TO 7-1 and 7-2 (July 15, 1943 and January 13, 1945) and TO 19-7 (July 15, 1943, March 28, 1944 and September 12, 1944). Changes after July 1943 appear in brackets.
1 Rifles were M1903 until December 10, 1943 when the issue of M1 rifles was authorized.
2 Only when authorized by the theater commander.
3 Two jeeps were for the chaplain section and one for the air-ground liaison officer (driven by a general staff section clerk). From January 1945, orderlies from the Special Platoon drove three other jeeps.
4 MP platoon enlarged as of September 12, 1944.
5 Section HQ (1-2); two (three) squads (0-11 each).
6 Section HQ (1-2); three (five) squads (0-11 each).

Tactics

The .45-cal M3 submachine gun was a lighter, lower cost replacement for the older Thompson submachine gun. It weighed about 8 lb. (2 1/2 lb. more than an M1 carbine and only 1 1/2 lb. less than an M1 rifle), had a slow cyclic rate of fire (350–450 rpm), and used a 30-round magazine.

US troops in France receive instruction in how to launch a grenade from an M1 rifle equipped with an M7 (or later) grenade launcher, July 14, 1944. The M7 grenade launcher could also launch 60mm mortar shells, as happened extensively during the siege of St. Nazaire.

Infantry tactical doctrine

By the beginning of 1944, the US Army had concluded that nothing in its previous combat experience suggested any need for significant changes to its tactical doctrine. Though the performance of the Army had not always been brilliant, apart from in the Philippines, it had generally been successful. Thus, the US Army continued to use its 1918-era French Army doctrine. This called for the destruction or the wearing down of the enemy with massive but carefully orchestrated firepower so that tanks and infantry could finish him off. The US Army saw this as sacrificing shells and bombs in place of its soldiers' lives. It oriented both its offense and defense towards the terrain rather than the enemy inasmuch as terrain was permanent and known while the enemy and his dispositions were often unknown and constantly changing. Combat units defended or attacked hills, towns, or other terrain features, and focused less on broader objectives that might have allowed more flexibility. Once they had attained their initial objectives, US soldiers too often failed to exploit their success. They preferred instead to wait for orders and supplies and to coordinate artillery support for the next attack. Except on the Pacific islands (where the Japanese could not retreat) this habit of delay meant that the US Army fought battles that were frequently successful but seldom decisive. The same enemies had to be fought again and again and this probably cost as many lives as the bombs and shells had saved.

The dominant (though not the only) tactical formation for the infantry in both attack and defense remained "two up, one back." This was a product of the triangular organization that the infantry used from platoon to division level. Triangular units had three main "maneuver" elements (weapons units did not count as "maneuver" elements). Rifle platoons had three squads; rifle companies, three rifle platoons; battalions, three rifle companies; and so forth. This encouraged commanders to place two of their maneuver units forward while keeping back the third so that it could relieve or reinforce a frontline unit. Special situations might call for other formations.

An M1919A6 LMG gunner fires his weapon through a hole in a wall at German troops in a barn 300 yards away, beyond Kohlsched, Germany, October 16, 1944.

During an advance, a unit might adopt a "wedge" formation with one element leading while the other two followed in line abreast. If the lead element encountered the enemy, the other two would still be free to maneuver. A unit might use a column formation, usually on a road or trail in terrain where off-road movement was difficult. A unit might also echelon itself to the left or right to protect a flank.

Weapons platoons and companies

Weapons platoons and companies served as the bases of fire for their parent companies and battalions, respectively. The rifle company weapons platoon light machine gun (LMG) section usually operated as a single element under the personal direction of the weapons platoon commander. Only on rare occasions was it attached to a rifle platoon. It delivered short- to medium-range fire, ideally from a flanking position that enabled it to fire across the entire front of the company. Late in the war the LMG sections began receiving the Browning .30-caliber LMG M1919A6. This was an M1919A4 with a bipod and shoulder stock that gave it better mobility and more utility in an assault. It could also fire from the same 14 lb. M2 tripod used by the M1919A4. However, the gun was heavy (32½ lb.) and awkward, and its light barrel rapidly overheated.

The 60mm mortar section, normally under the company commander's direct control, would fire (if possible) from a defilade position (any fold in the ground would do) about 500 yards behind the company frontline. The company commander or the mortar section leader chose the mortars' targets based more on what they could see than on any calls for fire from their rifle platoons. In theory the mortars were not supposed to use radios or field telephones lest they become too dependent on them. In practice, however, the mortar section made greater use of such equipment as the war progressed.

A soldier from the 4th Armored Division has just fired his bazooka, reportedly at a German gun emplacement, though neither he nor the M7 self-propelled howitzer to the left appear to be under fire; France, November 12, 1944. The late war bazooka was the M9. It was 61in. long and weighed 13.25 lb., but unlike its M1 predecessor could be broken in half for carrying. The effective range of the M6A1 or A3 3.4 lb. 2.36in. (60mm) rocket was out to 150–300 yards. Improvements to the warhead design increased armor penetration to 100–120mm. The standard crew was a gunner and a loader and they typically carried six rockets.

The weapons platoon's two jeeps with trailers served as weapons carriers. As such they carried the crew-served weapons (60mm mortars, LMG, .50-caliber MG and bazookas) and their ammunition. Weapons carriers rarely served as gun platforms. They existed to lighten the load of the weapon squads and increase their mobility. The crew-served weapons generally stayed in their carriers until reaching their "off carrier" positions. This was where the squads unloaded their weapons when combat was imminent. It would be as close as possible to the weapons' (preferably pre-selected) firing positions, while offering some cover and concealment. From there the squads would carry their weapons and an initial supply of ammunition to their initial firing positions leaving their weapons carriers with the reserve ammunition close by.

The weapons company was the base of fire for the whole battalion. In battle the two heavy machine-gun (HMG) platoons were supposed to work under the weapons company commander's control while the battalion commander directed the mortar platoon. In practice the battalion commander delegated control of the mortars back to the weapons company commander because he was too busy to direct them himself. Tactically, the M1917A1 HMG, which equipped the HMG platoons, was used like an M1919A4 LMG, but it was accurate to a much greater range (due to its heavy tripod). Being a water-cooled weapon, it could also maintain a much higher rate of fire. Each HMG or 81mm mortar squad had its own weapons carrier. The load per weapons carrier (weapon plus ammunition) was about 700 lb. for an HMG squad or 1,000 for a mortar squad. Since a jeep weapons carrier could carry only some of the squad members, an HMG or mortar platoon had to move in separate foot and motor echelons, except when enemy contact was expected.

In battle, the HMG platoons established observation posts from which the platoon instrument corporal determined ranges and the platoon leader or platoon sergeant selected reference points, identified targets, and adjusted fire. By 1944 the platoon was using field telephones rather than shouting and hand–arm signals to communicate between guns and observation posts. If the HMG platoon leader could not direct all the guns himself, he would delegate a section to his platoon sergeant. Most HMG fire missions were direct fire (meaning that the guns had a direct line of sight to their targets), but they could also fire indirectly and sometimes even over the heads of friendly troops. The HMG platoons tended to concentrate their fire on direct-fire heavy weapons behind the forward enemy positions. In the defense, HMG sections delivered flanking enfilade fire or a "final protective line" along the main line of resistance (MLR). The HMG platoon leaders also supervised the positioning of the rifle company LMG sections to ensure that they fitted into the overall battalion fire plan. Alternatively, the HMGs might be positioned in depth to block enemy penetrations. They might also occupy open positions forward of the MLR to deliver long-range harassing fire; however, as the enemy advanced, the HMG would withdraw to their primary firing positions behind the MLR.

The 81mm mortar platoon operated much like an HMG platoon with three sections but it had a harder time than the HMG platoon keeping its weapons supplied with ammunition. A mortar squad could fire off its 100 rounds or so in as little as 10 minutes. The mortars nearly always fired from defilade positions under the direction of nearby section- or platoon-level observation posts. During combat, if the mortars needed to displace, one section moved while the other two continued to fire. Like the 60mm mortars, the 81mm covered "dead space" inaccessible to other weapons, and it screened friendly movement with smoke or high explosives.

The Army saw mortars as particularly effective against entrenched crew-served weapons and targets in road cuts, behind railway embankments, and on reverse slopes. The mortar platoon leader kept in touch with the artillery observers and coordinated his fire with theirs. In offensive operations, the mortars would start at about 800 yards behind their frontlines and attack targets chosen for them by the battalion and weapons company commanders and the mortar platoon leader. The rifle companies would not have mortars attached to them unless the visibility was bad or the battalion very dispersed. In the defense, the mortars (either by sections or the whole platoon) started further back and attacked pre-planned locations that the enemy was expected to cross. With an officer section leader each mortar section could more easily operate independently. It could do its own fire direction and man up to two observation posts (one per squad). Independent firing by sections was better for distributing fire across the battalion frontline and filling the gaps in coverage that the artillery left.

Infantry regiment cannon and antitank companies

The commander of the cannon company was responsible for the training and supply of his company and for advising the regimental commander on how best to use the cannon platoons. The platoons themselves operated independently under their parent regimental commander's control. The platoon leaders and the reconnaissance officer chose firing positions for the guns and (together with the section chiefs) the placement of observation posts (OPs). Each gun section could deploy an observation post consisting of the section chief and one cannoneer serving as a wireman (with a CE-11 reel unit and sound-powered phone connected to the guns). The platoon leader could form his own OP but usually chose to co-locate with the OP of one of his sections. If there was a place for an OP that could observe most or all of the platoon sector, the platoon might operate only one OP. The platoon sergeant was left in charge of the guns and vehicles. Normally, one cannon platoon supported each forward-deployed infantry battalion in the regiment. Since one battalion was usually kept back, its cannon platoon reinforced one of the other platoons or temporarily assumed its mission while it displaced to a new firing position.

Although the guns in a cannon platoon could operate separately, each platoon tried to keep both its guns together and firing at the same targets. The cannon platoons were also supposed to deliver direct fire; however, direct fire was dangerous, and the M3 howitzers were ill suited to it. Most cannon platoon missions were indirect fire and differed little from missions fired by the division artillery except that they involved far fewer weapons. The cannon platoons operated in much the same ways as the 81mm mortar sections operated within the infantry battalion.

A T-12 self-propelled gun, consisting of a 75mm field gun mounted on an M3 half-track, emerges from the woods during a training exercise in England, October 28, 1942. The T-12 (or M3) equipped infantry regimental cannon companies until late 1943 when the towed M3 105mm howitzer officially replaced it. However, it continued to serve in a few units.

An M7 self-propelled howitzer crosses a bridge built by the 36th Engineer Regiment near Remiremont, France on September 24, 1944. Although the M7 was normally found within the armored divisions or separate self-propelled artillery battalions, it also equipped the cannon companies in a number of infantry regiments.

Members of the Cannon Company, 101st Infantry (26th Division) clean and grease a 105mm M3 howitzer in a photo taken in either France or Germany, October 17, 1944. The man on the left is probably the gunner. The man on the right appears to be the platoon artillery mechanic. Originally designed for airborne use, the M3 weighed 2,495 lb., used a Chevrolet G7107 or 7117 as prime mover, and fired the same shells as the M2A1 howitzers in the division artillery; however, its range was only 8,295 yards.

The regimental antitank company and the battalion antitank platoons supplied only minimal antitank protection to the regiment. To counter a serious tank threat required the use of tank destroyers, which had to come from echelons above the division. The antitank company commander, who was also the regimental antitank officer, usually deployed his platoons to cover roads and other likely armor avenues of approach. He left the exact placement of the guns to his platoon commanders and reconnaissance officer. The antitank mine platoon reinforced the gun platoons with antitank minefields. The mine platoon (and the battalion pioneer platoons) could also remove mines. However, the antitank company grew less effective as the war went on. Its new M1 57mm gun, though more powerful than the previous M3 37mm, had by mid 1944 become inadequate against the heavier German tanks. No real attempt was made to upgrade the 57mm gun because the number of German tanks encountered was steadily shrinking and tank destroyers and fighter-bombers were deemed adequate to counter them. By late 1944 antitank platoons were leaving their guns behind and substituting extra bazookas, but during the Battle of the Bulge many units discovered the hard way that they really needed their guns after all.

The division artillery

Under US Army doctrine the artillery of an infantry division constituted its base of fire and much of its combat power. An artillery battalion that was part of or attached to the division artillery might serve in a direct support (DS), general support (GS), or reinforcing role. A DS battalion was almost always organic to a division and directly associated with an infantry regiment. It fired all its missions in support of that regiment. A GS battalion, typically under the direct control of the division artillery commander, fired in support of the division as a whole. Because a division frontline was usually too wide for its single 155mm GS battalion to cover, attached 155mm battalions had to plug the gaps. Since a division seldom had more than two of its regiments in contact with the enemy at any one time the DS battalion with the unengaged regiment would fire in either a GS role or to reinforce the fire of another GS or DS battalion. Battalions attached to the division artillery usually fired in a GS or reinforcing role. Under US doctrine artillery was never kept in reserve.

Earlier in the war artillery fire missions were usually pre-planned, but as communications improved and the number of forward observer (FO) parties increased, many more missions were fired against targets of opportunity and directed by an observer. However, a target was only engaged on the order of the artillery commander or his liaison officer.

Every artillery battalion headquarters battery included a fire direction center (FDC). Artillery tactics relied on massed fire. Most fire missions were battalion sized or larger and the battalion FDC computed firing data for all its howitzer batteries. The goal was to blanket the target with as many shells as possible before the target could move away or take cover. An artillery battalion was much more efficient at this than a single battery. Though the division artillery headquarters battery lacked an FDC it could still coordinate the fire of two or more battalions on a common target.

A field artillery battalion or higher-level observation post belonging to the 80th Division operates from a World War I monument near Kontaec, France in September 1944. The officer in the center is using a "BC" or battery commander's scope, a combination telescope, range finder, and direction finder. A man on the right uses an EE-8 field telephone. The monument would probably have been marked on German maps, and the observation party thus risks receiving German counter-fire.

A howitzer battery did not have an FDC, but it could improvise one if necessary. A DS battery was usually associated with one of the battalions of the infantry regiment that its parent battalion supported. It would operate its FO team and observation post (OP) in the sector of that battalion when it was in the frontline. By 1944 commanders understood that infantry units moved in and out of the line often enough and unexpectedly enough that artillery observers had to be with them at all times. It was best to attach an FO team to each rifle company. This meant that an infantry battalion needed three teams and its associated DS battery was allowed only one. Therefore, the DS battery had to improvise the other two. Typically, the assistant battery executive officer would head one improvised FO team while the battery reconnaissance sergeant headed the other.

In addition, the battalion headquarters battery sent a liaison team to each infantry battalion. The liaison team coordinated the artillery fire with the operations of that battalion.

Artillerymen lay telephone wire with an RL-31 reel unit mounted on the bed of a 3/4-ton truck, south of Villersexel, France, September 18, 1944.

The pilot of an L-4 Field Artillery observation aircraft boards his plane at an improvised airstrip in Germany on December 11, 1944. A berm erected around the aircraft protects it from enemy fire.

Since October 1942 the headquarters batteries of each artillery battalion and the division artillery included a pair of slow and unarmed, but stable and reliable, liaison aircraft. Most were L-4 "Piper Cubs" or L-5 "Stinson Sentinels." They observed, acquired targets (especially enemy artillery), and directed fire. The 10 aircraft per division artillery typically based themselves on the same level field or straight stretch of road (they required very little takeoff and landing space), and operated as a de facto squadron. After September 1944 they did so under the direction of the division artillery air operations officer. The planes flew continuous daylight patrols and battalion commanders could easily request their services. To ensure their own survival the planes only operated at low altitude, avoided enemy territory, and quickly made themselves scarce whenever enemy fighters were detected.

When an artillery battalion had to displace itself in combat, it moved only one battery at a time (preceded by a reconnaissance party to select its new firing position). The other two batteries continued to fire. A battery was vulnerable to both ground and air attack. Its trucks, unless stationary and well camouflaged, were easy to spot. The carbines that most of its men carried lacked stopping power. The slow practical rate of fire of their .50-caliber machine guns limited their effect against foot troops. However, bazookas and special HEAT (high-explosive antitank) shells for the 105mm howitzers provided some protection against enemy armor.

Artillerymen from an unidentified artillery battalion in France deliver "high-angle" fire (more than 45° elevation) from their M2A1 105mm howitzer on November 12, 1944. High-angle fire was normally used to clear a nearby obstacle, presumably the trees in the background. The gunners have dug a pit below the breech of the howitzer so it does not recoil into the ground. The M2A1 was a heavy (4,980 lb.) weapon, but was rugged, accurate, and highly successful. It could fire its standard high-explosive (HE) shell to 12,200 yards at up to 10 rounds per minute. It even had a shaped-charge antitank shell that could defeat up to 115mm of armor, though its accurate range in direct fire could not have been more than 1,000 yards. For further details, see Battle Orders 17, *US Army Infantry Divisions 1942–43*.

Combat engineers

The primary mission of the division combat engineer battalion was to enhance the mobility of its parent division and impair the mobility of its opponents. It did this by breaching or erecting natural or manmade obstacles such as minefields, rivers, and roadblocks. It also built or repaired roads and bridges for the use of its division or destroyed or blocked them to hinder or prevent enemy use. It could also support a river crossing, but only if higher headquarters made boats, rafts, and bridging material available.

The engineer battalion normally worked as a single entity directly under division control. In most combat situations higher headquarters would reinforce each division with two or three additional engineer battalions. These additional battalions normally worked further to the rear building roads or bridges. The division did not normally attach combat engineer companies to its infantry regiments, except very briefly or when the latter were detached from the division and serving (together with its associated DS artillery battalion) as separate regimental combat teams (RCTs).

The infantry regiments had limited combat engineering capabilities of their own in the form of their antitank mine and pioneer platoons.

One of the most useful tools the engineers had was the "medium tractor crawler type with angle-dozer," or D7-series bulldozer. It was especially valuable for road building, debris removal, and burying enemy pillboxes. It could also clear obstacles but explosives were often better for this. The bulldozer itself was usually a commercial model, sometimes with an armored cab. It could not move far on its tracks so a 4-ton truck with 8-ton semi-trailer was made ready to transport it.

Laying and clearing minefields was mostly done by hand. Special mine-clearing tanks existed but an infantry division engineer battalion was not likely to see one. The division G-3 (see *Command, control, communications, and intelligence*), the engineer battalion commander, and the commander of the infantry regiment in whose sector the mines were to be used planned and coordinated most mine-laying tasks. The regimental antitank mine platoon and pioneer platoons could perform most of the work under engineer direction. Mine clearing was trickier and usually required the use of explosives. The engineers had to do more of that work themselves, although the pioneers and antitank mine platoons did have their own mine detectors and could assist.

In offensive combat, the engineers normally fought as squad-sized obstacle-breaching teams. They did not normally fight as infantry because they lacked the mortars, light automatic weapons, and light radios they would have needed to be really effective. When engineers did fight as infantry, it was usually in the defense, since they were relatively well equipped with machine guns. Typically an engineer company would fight as an attachment to an infantry battalion while relying on it for mortars and tactical communications.

Engineers from the 319th Combat Engineer Battalion, 94th Division, prepare to destroy a roadblock with TNT charges, February 21, 1945.

Two members of the 202nd Combat Engineer Battalion man a .50-cal machine gun to protect their comrades as they build a bridge across the Roer River, February 26, 1945. The M2 .50-cal machine gun was a powerful, sturdy, and popular weapon but it was heavy, and over-heated rapidly. It had a practical rate of fire of 40–60 rounds per minute.

Tanks and antitank support

It was only in the European Theater of Operations (ETO) that tank, tank destroyer, and antiaircraft automatic weapons battalions were routinely attached to infantry divisions. This was a result of experience in the Normandy campaign. The hope was that tank or tank destroyer battalions would remain associated with a division for long enough to get used to working with it as a team. A tank battalion, with its 60 medium (six with 105mm howitzers and the rest with 75 or 76mm guns) and 17 light tanks, was a powerful force, though its light tanks had only limited utility. In the offensive, an infantry division commander was likely to parcel out his tank battalion's three medium companies among his three infantry regiments while keeping the light tank company in reserve or attaching it to his reconnaissance troop. In the defense, he was more likely to keep his tank battalion together so that it could spearhead a counterattack force.

Although powerfully armed with 76 or 90mm guns the tank destroyers were of less utility than tanks. There were only 36 tank destroyers per battalion. Although they were usually self-propelled their light armor meant that they had to be used carefully. They could rarely spearhead attacks but they were, however, very valuable as direct fire support weapons.

The main difficulty with the tank battalions and, to a lesser extent, tank destroyers was that there were never enough of them. Only 37 tank battalions (two with only light tanks) supported the 42 infantry divisions that fought in France and Germany. There were 56 tank destroyer battalions but the infantry divisions had to share these with 15 armored divisions and (for brief periods) two or more airborne divisions. The result was that tank and tank destroyer battalions were frequently switching from divisions that needed them to other divisions that needed them even more. This tended to undermine the continuity and cohesion possible with the same tank or tank destroyer operating with the same division.

On the other hand, more than 170 antiaircraft battalions operated in France and Germany of which 53 were antiaircraft gun battalions (sixteen 90mm guns

An M10 tank destroyer crosses a stream marking the German border, near Hammeras, while another M10 approaches, September 12, 1944. Tank destroyers were not organic to any infantry division but 57 tank destroyer battalions (most of them self-propelled) served in the European Theater and many were attached to infantry divisions. The M10 was the most common tank destroyer. It carried a fairly powerful 3in. gun (converted from an antiaircraft weapon) in an open-topped turret. Its light armor precluded its use as a tank.

A US tank (probably a 75mm-armed M4A3) fires point blank at a target in Aachen, Germany, October 15, 1944. Wary American infantrymen take cover in the doorways.

each). These were rarely (if ever) attached to infantry divisions. The rest were automatic weapons battalions (each with 32 single 37mm or 40mm and 32 multiple-mounted .50-caliber guns). Only 24 were self-propelled (using M3 series armored half-tracks) and most of them served with the armored divisions. The rest were towed. Some battalions were attached to divisions to defend their forward areas. Others served further back. Given that the Allied air forces outnumbered the Luftwaffe by seven to one (or more) throughout the fighting in Western Europe, one wonders why the US Army spent so much of its scarce manpower on so many antiaircraft battalions.

An M24 light tank from the 117th Cavalry Reconnaissance Squadron fires during range practice in the St. Jean Saverne area, France, March 9, 1945.

Three crew members of an M20 armored utility car of the 878th Tank Destroyer Battalion (attached to the 26th Division) search the upper Saar River near Serrig, Germany for signs of enemy activity, March 15, 1945. The M20 was an M8 armored car with its turret removed. It carried a ring-mounted .50-cal machine gun. Its main function was as a command vehicle with radios and a folding map table. It could accommodate up to six passengers besides its two-man crew. An infantry division was allowed one M20 for the division commander — and then only if the theater commander approved it.

Brigadier General William F. Dean of Salt Lake City, UT, then assistant commander of the 44th Infantry Division, inspects an M1 57mm antitank gun (possibly one of those in the division headquarters company defense platoon) in Herbitzheim, France, January 24, 1945. The M1 57mm antitank gun weighed 2,810 lb. in action. Its standard armor-piercing shot could defeat 73mm of homogeneous armor at 20° at 1,000 yards. Five and a half years later Dean, by then a major general commanding the 24th Division, would become the highest-ranking American to be taken prisoner by Communist forces in Korea.

Command, control, communications, and intelligence

Command and control

Where command and control was a matter of personal contact, generally at the platoon level or below, it was a simple function performed with arm and hand signals and voice commands. Leaders at these levels usually had assistants to extend their span of control and to take over for them if they became casualties. Combat companies (such as rifle, weapons, antitank, or cannon companies) had relatively large headquarters that, for combat, operated as forward and rear command posts (CPs). The forward CP exerted tactical control over the company. It consisted of the company commander and all or most of the company's communication and reconnaissance personnel. The rear CP, headed by the company executive officer or first sergeant, performed mainly supply, administration and "housekeeping" tasks. Many of its members were not physically present with the company but worked on its behalf with other elements of the regiment. The rear CP could command the company if the forward CP could not.

All units of battalion size and larger had headquarters companies (or in certain cases headquarters detachments). Headquarters companies housed the enlisted men serving with the battalion (or larger) headquarters, the communications platoon, and special units of less than company size. Since a headquarters company did not fight as a unit it did not organize a forward CP. Its commander looked after training, logistics, administration, and local security but did not exercise tactical command and control.

Battalion and larger headquarters followed a system copied from the French during 1918. The French had developed it mainly for division-level headquarters and higher. The system divided the core of any headquarters into several theoretically co-equal sections to achieve clearer lines of responsibility and (in theory) more efficient work. The first section was for personnel and administrative matters, the second for intelligence, the third for training and

Lieutenant General George S. Patton's personal command car with its .50-cal machine gun and M31 mount and armor plating against mines, photographed in England, March 1944.

operations, and the fourth for logistics. Instead of restricting the system to division and higher levels as the French intended, the US Army applied it down to the battalion level. This was because ill-trained and inexperienced American commanders in World War I had great difficulty operating with the very small staffs that French and German commanders found adequate. However, instead of training its own officers to do what French and German officers did, the US Army simply created larger staffs and followed the theory that several heads are better than one. Although large staffs can produce orders and decisions, the need for internal consensus and coordination slows them down, as it does any bureaucracy. This led to slower reaction times, missed opportunities and a tendency to favor slow-moving, firepower-intensive, "set-piece" battles.

The Army designated its staff sections (and their section heads) with a letter and a number. At the division level and higher they all used the letter "G" and at the regiment and battalion levels they used "S." Thus, the head of a division's intelligence section, for example, was the G-2. In a battalion or regiment he would be the S-2, and so forth.

Despite this imitation of the French system, an infantry battalion headquarters in 1943 was still fairly small. It consisted of only: the battalion commander, executive officer, S-2, and S-3. In practice the executive officer doubled as S-3 while the nominal S-3 served as his assistant. Likewise, the headquarters company commander doubled as S-1. The regimental S-1 and the staff section of the regimental service company performed most of the regiment's administrative tasks so there was relatively little for a battalion S-1 to do. The regimental service company also supplied each battalion with an S-4. The battalion headquarters section of the headquarters company supplied enlisted assistants for the S-2 and S-3.

An infantry regimental headquarters was similar to that of a battalion but its section heads had higher ranks and its S-3 was really the S-3. The S-4 and the enlisted assistants for all sections except the S-2 belonged to the service company. The full-time S-1 had (and he needed) a warrant officer assistant. The regiment's three liaison officers served with the headquarters of the division and its other two infantry regiments. They kept the division commander informed of events happening elsewhere in the division.

The division headquarters consisted of a series of sections. Some of these, such as the adjutant general (administration and postal), inspector general, judge advocate general, and finance sections, performed special functions. Others offered special expertise or planning and coordination for their specific service branches. The core of the division headquarters was the general staff section. Headed by the division chief of staff (a colonel) it included the G-1, G-2, G-3, and G-4 officers (all lieutenant colonels) and both their officer and enlisted assistants. This section actually planned and supervised the operations of the division. The other sections played only supporting roles.

Each infantry division commander had one of these five-passenger sedans.

At the Amphibious Training Center at Camp Gordon Johnston, FL in February 1943, a T-5 technician demonstrates the awkward SCR-511 radio, originally designed for use by cavalrymen on horseback. The far superior SCR-300 replaced the SCR-511 during 1944. For further details see Battle Orders 17, *US Army Infantry Divisions 1942–43*.

At the Amphibious Training Center at Camp Gordon Johnston, FL an SCR-610 is photographed mounted on a jeep.

Inasmuch as it did not operate so close to the enemy the division artillery experienced fewer command and control problems than the infantry did. Its headquarters and headquarters battery was its main interface with division headquarters. The division artillery commander participated in division-level planning, and served as artillery advisor to the division commander. He chose the general locations where his battalions would operate and assigned them their missions, ordering necessary changes as the battle unfolded. The headquarters battery could also coordinate fire from two or more battalions onto the same target. The survey and meteorological sections improved artillery accuracy with exact positional and weather data.

Artillery battalion headquarters and their headquarters batteries were the most important link within the division artillery chain of command. They positioned their subordinate howitzer batteries, chose their targets, calculated their firing data, and coordinated their supply. The direct support battalions also worked closely with the infantry regiments through the artillery battalion liaison sections and forward observers.

Communication equipment

In 1944, tactical communication in all the major armies was either by telephone, messenger, radio, or visual signal. Messengers were secure and reliable but slow. Visual signals required clear weather and were also slow. Field telephones were secure and much more rapid. They could transmit not only voice messages but with telegraph sets and "buzzer" phones could also transmit even more rapidly and securely using Morse code. Although the wire cables made a telephone network reliable and secure, it was arduous and time consuming to lay them. Once laid, the wire was easily cut by artillery fire and passing vehicles. Burying the wire eased but did not solve this problem and, of course, made the process of laying wire a much slower one.

Radios did not require cable but were subject to the effects of unreliable batteries, variable atmospheric conditions, jamming, direction finding, and interception. In addition to voice messages, radios could transmit Morse code messages faster and over longer distances by using continuous wave (CW) or (in a few cases) tone mode. The M-209 cipher device could encrypt and decrypt Morse messages for secure transmission. Every battalion or regimental communication platoon message center had two of them. Although the Germans were eventually able to read M-209 messages, and although encryption and decryption with the M-209 approximately tripled message transmission time, the Signal Corps regarded the M-209 as sufficient for tactical use and did not replace it until after the Korean War.

The campaign in North Africa saw the first use of radios using frequency modulation (FM) rather than the more traditional amplitude modulation (AM). The first FM sets were heavy ones intended for vehicular use. Lighter man-packed sets (like the SCR-300) did not see combat until the Anzio landings of January 1944 and US forces were still using many AM sets at the end of the war. The advantage of an FM set was that it had far less static. Its transmissions were much easier to hear and understand. FM was a revolutionary technology that only US forces had.

Nevertheless, the unreliability and insecurity inherent in radio transmissions made it desirable to use other communication means whenever possible. Telephone remained the preferred method but as radios improved their use gradually increased, especially in offensive operations when there was little or no time for laying cable.

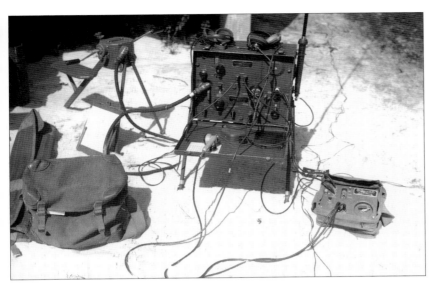

At the Amphibious Training Center at Camp Gordon Johnston, FL this SCR-284 medium-range radio is configured for ground operation; its spare parts bag is to the left and its power unit to the right.

Although shown here mounted in a jeep, the SCR-499 radio would normally reside in a 2^1/$_2$-ton truck. A jeep offered little operating space, could scarcely bear the weight of the radio, and was too light to tow the PE-95 generator in its heavy trailer. (Photo taken at Camp Polk, LA, January 28, 1944.)

A WC-56 or 57 ^{3}/$_4$-ton command and reconnaissance (C&R) truck carries an SCR-608 multi-channel field artillery type transmitter and receiver. The device on top of the radio is an RM-29B remote unit that connected the radio to a field telephone line. It enabled an operator to modulate the transmitter or hear the receiver from many miles away by using a field telephone. The rifles are both M1903. (Image taken at Ft Monmouth, NJ, 1943.)

The official caption of this photo says it shows an infantry patrol from the 4th Infantry Division looking for snipers in the town of Libin, Belgium on September 7, 1944. However, judging by the number and types of radios, it is more likely that it depicts a rifle company headquarters. The soldier on the left carries a bazooka and a carbine. The one on the right carries an SCR-300 backpack radio. An SCR-536 hand-held radio rests on the ground.

This six-line 45 lb. (supposedly lightweight) BD-71 switchboard was the sole telephone switchboard for an infantry battalion. It and the 75 lb. BD-72 (12 lines) also served in the infantry regimental communication platoon. For a complete listing of US Army field telephone equipment see Battle Orders 17, *US Army Infantry Divisions 1942–43*.

Communication architecture

All infantry units of company size or larger maintained their own radio networks. Rifle and weapons companies were each allowed six SCR-536 lightweight hand-held radios (see Table 3, page 44). The company commander decided who would get the radios but normally he gave one to each platoon leader and the company CP. He kept one for his own use when he was not in the CP. In a weapons company one radio would also go to the reconnaissance officer. Because only a technician could adjust the frequency of an SCR-536, an SCR-536 belonging to one company could not normally communicate with an SCR-536 from another. In order to talk to his rifle and weapons companies, a battalion commander (through his communication officer) would issue each of them a man-packed SCR-300 FM radio. The company had to find its own operator. The radio section of the battalion communication platoon kept two SCR-300s to talk to the companies (one for the CP and the other for the battalion commander) and a heavier, longer-ranged SCR-284 (or 694s) for communication with regimental headquarters. The radio section of the regimental communication platoon had eight SCR-300s and six SCR-284s (or 694) with which to link the regiment's three battalions and its service, antitank, and cannon companies. The regimental intelligence and reconnaissance platoon had four more SCR-300s. The service company had no radio or telephone equipment and the cannon company had no SCR-284 (or 694) to link it with regimental headquarters. Both these companies depended on the regimental communication platoon to supply the equipment and operators they needed.

The division artillery used radio mainly for communication between batteries and with forward observer and liaison teams. The artillery used relatively few radios and most were "portable." A "portable" radio could operate from the ground, but was too heavy to carry very far. A genuine man-pack artillery radio was unavailable for forward observers until the SCR-619 appeared in 1944. The engineers used radios mainly for communication outside the battalion or with detached companies. In 1944 they exchanged their lighter man-packed types for a much smaller number of longer-ranged portable sets.

In the infantry (except the rifle and weapons companies), telephone networks generally duplicated radio networks. EE-8 battery-powered telephones connected by heavy W-110 or lightweight W-130 wire through BD-71 and 72 switchboards were standard for telephone networks. However, simpler, shorter-ranged networks (such as those connecting observation or listening posts or weapon pits to a company or platoon headquarters) typically used CE-11 reel units (each with only 1/4-mile of W-130 wire) and sound-powered telephones.

For wire equipment a rifle company rated only two CE-11 reel units. This was hardly enough to link the company commander with his 60mm mortars or perhaps an outpost or two. A weapons company, on the other hand, had enough telephone equipment to connect all its crew-served weapons, platoon headquarters, and observation posts with company headquarters. For internal communication, rifle companies relied on messengers. These usually worked in pairs. A platoon commander, for example, would station one of his two messengers with his company commander and keep the other with himself. When he needed to send a message he would send his messenger to company headquarters. That messenger would remain at company headquarters and send the other back with the reply. Messengers had to be intelligent and resourceful, and able to read maps and find their way after dark. Messengers near the front were always on foot but those further back used bicycles, motorcycles or jeeps.

Battalion and higher-level headquarters (in the infantry and artillery) all had communication platoons. All were organized in essentially the same way, differing from one another mainly in scale. The hub of any communication unit was its message center. Message center clerks wrote outgoing messages in triplicate using a special message pad with carbon pages. The message center chief sent all messages by the fastest or most secure means, be it by radio, telephone, messenger, or a visual signal. When receiving incoming messages the message center clerks logged them and then had them delivered to their addressees.

The largest and busiest element of a communication platoon was its wire or telephone section. Whenever its parent unit halted, the section would start building a telephone network and continuously expanded, improved, and repaired it. The section used vehicles with reel units to lay the telephone wire whenever possible. When it was time to move again the section had to scramble to recover, clean, and rewind its wire (even rich Americans could not afford to abandon a lot of wire), and secure its other gear.

Despite their reliability problems and vulnerability to jamming and interception, radios were an essential communication means for any unit without a telephone network. However, if an effective telephone network were in place radio section personnel could act as visual signalers. Because of the highly technical nature of their duties about two-thirds of all radio operators (nearly all after mid 1944) in tactical units held technician rank (usually T-4 or T-5).

The division artillery used wire whenever possible for communication within its howitzer and headquarters batteries. The battalion communication platoon was also wire dependent. When there was time wire might also serve to connect batteries with liaison teams and observation posts.

The division signal company was the hub of the division communication network. Actual communication was the function of the company's operations platoon. The construction platoon built and maintained the division's telephone network but did not operate it. The headquarters platoon provided maintenance, administration, and logistical support. Like a regimental or battalion communication platoon the operations platoon had its radio and message center sections. The radio section operated only a small number of large vehicle-mounted sets but could man them 24 hours a day. Its SCR-299 (later 399 or 499) was the largest and longest-ranged set in the division and maintained contact with corps headquarters and other divisions. The SCR-193 radios were for long-range

An EE-8 field telephone, shown here with its ringing equipment, batteries, and leather case, was the US Army's standard field telephone. Its talking range using W-110 wire was 14 miles. Using lightweight W-130 wire restricted its range to about five miles.

A long-ranged SCR-193 (right) and a short-ranged SCR-510 (left) are shown mounted in an M-2 half-track in Northern Ireland, July 6, 1942. Both radio types were used by the reconnaissance troop until the SCR-506 replaced the SCR-193. After that the SCR-193 only served in the division signal company and the division artillery. The SCR-193 could communicate with aircraft as well as ground stations.

Table 3: Infantry division radio equipment (1944–45)

System (year in service)	Freq band (MHz)	Power output (watts)	Modulation	Mode of operation and range (miles)	Normal mode of transport	Power source	Weight (lb.)	Notes
SCR-193	1.5–4.5	50	AM	60 (CW) 40 (tone) 20 (voice)	Vehicle	Rotary/vibrator converter or dry batteries	240	(1)
SCR-284	3.8–5.8	25 CW 12 AM	AM	30 (CW) 20 (tone) 15 (voice)	Vehicle or portable	Dry batteries, hand generator, or vibrator converter	250	(2)
SCR-299 SCR-399 SCR-499	2–8 2–18 2–18	400 CW 300 AM	AM	95 (voice) c.150 (CW)	2¹/₂-ton truck with trailer	AC generator (PE-95)	6,500	(3)
SCR-300 SCR-619	40–48 27–38.9	0.5	FM	3 (reliable) or 20 (nominal)	Man-pack	Dry batteries	38	(4)
SCR-506	2–4.5	50	FM	50 (CW) 25 (voice)	Vehicle	Rotary/vibrator converter	530	(5)
SCR-508 SCR-528	20–27.9	25	FM	10 (voice)	Vehicle	Rotary/vibrator converter	200 Under 200	(6)
SCR-510 SCR-610	20–27.9 27–38.9	1.3	FM	5 (voice)	Portable or vehicle	Vibrator converter PE-97 power unit	120	(7)
SCR-536	3.5–6	0.02	AM	1 (voice)	Man portable	Dry batteries	6	(8)
SCR-608	27–38.9	35	FM	15 (voice)	Vehicle	Rotary/vibrator converter or dry batteries	200	(9)
SCR-694	3.8–5.8	25 CW 8.5 AM	AM	30+ (CW) 20 (tone) 15 (voice)	Vehicle or portable	Dry batteries, hand generator, or vibrator converter	192	(10)

Notes: Only the more common types before 1944 are shown above. Transmission ranges apply when both transmitting and receiving stations are stationary. Movement by either or both stations could reduce transmission ranges by up to half. Unless otherwise noted each radio consisted of either a single transceiver or one transmitter and one receiver.

(1) Heavy medium-range HF vehicular radio used by the division signal company and (after March 1944) the artillery.

(2) Used for battalion-level and higher communication; could be mounted in a vehicle or used from the ground. For ground operation one man operated the radio while another operated the generator. It was in general use by mid 1943 but proved to be too heavy and fragile in combat. The SCR-694 replaced it.

(3) This was a high-power, long-range radio system with one transmitter and two receivers for division level or higher use. The SCR-299 was mounted on a special K-51 2¹/₂-ton truck. The SCR-399 and 499 were mounted in vans that any 2¹/₂-ton cargo truck could carry. The truck towed a K-52 trailer with a PU-95 generator. The SCR-299 served successfully in North Africa and Sicily but the others began to replace it after that.

(4) This was the US Army's first purpose-designed, man-pack FM voice radio. It served with great success, first seeing combat at Anzio in January 1944 and also served throughout the Korean War. The SCR-619 was the artillery version.

(5) This vehicular radio set replaced the SCR-193 as the long-range radio for the infantry division's M8 armored cars.

(6) This was the first FM radio to see combat. In the infantry division it was the shorter-ranged radio for the M8 armored cars in the reconnaissance troop. It had two receivers so it could monitor two frequencies but the lighter SCR-528 had only one receiver. Although it could be used from the ground, its weight normally dictated vehicular use.

(7) Short-range vehicular radio, the artillery version (SCR-610) was also portable. SCR-510 operated from jeeps in the division reconnaissance troop. Both the SCR-510 and SCR-610 were also used for air-ground communication by liaison aircraft. The battery-powered portable version was the SCR-509 (armor) or SCR-609 (artillery).

(8) Lightweight device used for communication within rifle and weapons companies. Introduced in 1942; first combat use was in 1943.

(9) This was a medium-range artillery radio closely related to the armored force's SCR-508. It had a more powerful transmitter but only one receiver.

(10) This unit was a lighter, sturdier and more reliable late-war replacement for the less-than-successful SCR-284. Its ability to receive commercial radio stations made it very popular with the troops.

A rear view of what is probably an SCR-299 transmitter and receiver unit mounted on the bed of a 2½-ton truck near Camp Young, Desert Training Center, CA, November 21, 1942.

communication within the division. Early in the war the radio section began to attach a ¾-ton truck with an SCR-193 to each infantry regiment and another to the division artillery so they could better communicate with division headquarters. In order to support this practice the War Department increased the number of SCR-193 from five to eight at the end of 1943 and gave the division artillery an SCR-193 of its own in early 1944. The radio and wire sections also provided communication support not only to division headquarters but also to the quartermaster and ordnance companies (which had no communication assets of their own) and to the medical battalion (which lost its radios in July 1944). The signal company's many commitments caused it to be the only element of the infantry division (besides the military police platoon) to actually increase in size between mid 1943 and the end of the war.

Intelligence

Although every soldier was expected to collect and report information that might be processed into useful intelligence, relatively few did intelligence or reconnaissance work on anything like a full-time basis. An infantry battalion had only a lieutenant (S-2), a sergeant, and six scout-observers. The scout-observers could provide expertise in scouting and patrolling to the rifle companies, man observation posts, and accompany patrols.

An infantry regimental commander had a major as his S-2 together with an intelligence and reconnaissance (I&R) platoon. The I&R platoon worked directly for the regimental commander and S-2 as their "eyes and ears." Its headquarters doubled as the S-2 office staff and its two squads, both fully motorized, could conduct motor or foot patrols, observe, and operate either independently or in conjunction with other units. They could reconnoiter terrain as well as the enemy. They were seldom if ever attached to any battalion. Their armament was strictly defensive. They were not expected to fight for information. Generally, an I&R patrol would be of at least squad size and include at least one SCR-300 radio for rapid reporting of information.

The division artillery relied on its forward observers, observation posts, liaison teams, and spotter aircraft to keep it informed of the current situation. Batteries sent out ad hoc patrols to reconnoiter their route prior to moving from one position to the next. The engineer battalion also had a small reconnaissance section, for route reconnaissance and to assess construction or demolition jobs prior to the arrival of a working party.

Members of the Intel and Recon (I&R) Platoon of the 60th Infantry, 9th Infantry Division have rigged a pair of bazookas on a machine gun mount to give their jeep an antitank weapon. They have improvised some armor for their vehicle as well. In battle the jeep would carry a third man to load the bazookas. This photo is dated January 12, 1945.

PFC Wallace Grant from Laveen, AZ was a full-blooded Pima Indian and a former member of the US Olympic track team who was to have competed at the canceled 1940 Olympics in Helsinki, Finland. He is shown here serving as a runner bringing back a message from a scouting patrol near Arawe, New Britain, January 25, 1944.

McNair had not been in favor of a division-level reconnaissance unit. He believed that between foot patrols from the rifle companies, the regimental I&R platoons, and corps-level cavalry reconnaissance squadrons (battalions) there were too many levels of reconnaissance already. Nevertheless, in 1941 the War Department authorized a cavalry reconnaissance troop (company) for each infantry division. The combat theaters wanted a squadron per division but the AGF overruled them on the grounds that an infantry division did not operate on a broad enough frontage to justify one. Determining the best way to organize the reconnaissance troop involved much trial and error. In early 1943, McNair proposed his own cavalry troop. The troop headquarters was enlarged to include a liaison section (to accompany division headquarters) and extra mechanics (to replace squadron-level maintenance). Each reconnaissance platoon had an armored car section with long-range radios and a scout section (with jeeps). The armored cars acted as the base of fire (though their armor and firepower were often inadequate for this) while the jeeps did the scouting. Three jeeps per scout section carried 60mm mortars, mainly for laying smoke to assist the platoon in breaking contact with any enemy they might encounter. However, the scout section was too small to man its mortars effectively and the range and payload of 60mm mortar ammunition was inadequate. Since motor vehicles were available to carry both mortars and their ammunition, there was no reason not to use a heavier mortar. Before the war ended the reconnaissance troops in the First and Third armies in France and Germany replaced their 60mm mortars with one 81mm per scout section, and this proved to be much more satisfactory.

The training of the reconnaissance troops emphasized the gathering of information while avoiding enemy contact. However, actual combat experience vindicated McNair's view that a division reconnaissance troop would seldom be needed for reconnaissance. Instead, reconnaissance troops mainly executed such traditional cavalry missions as screening their parent division's front or a flank, countering enemy reconnaissance, or preventing surprise. They also provided rear security and even engaged in conventional offensive or defensive combat. In the attack the reconnaissance platoons usually fought mounted but in the defense the scout section routinely dismounted most of its men. However, there were seldom enough dismounted men to engage in close combat. Most reconnaissance troops acquired a BAR per scout section so that each scout section would have an automatic weapon that it could use while dismounted.

Logistics

An early production Diamond-T model 968A four-ton 6x6 truck photographed at Ft Holabird, MD in November 1941. In July 1943 an infantry division rated 18 of these trucks (15 for the 155mm howitzer battalion and three with the engineer battalion). Later in the war M5 tractors usually replaced the trucks with the artillery battalion. A 4-ton truck had a curb weight of 18,400 lb. and a gross weight of 26,400. It could carry an optional 15,000 lb. winch. For more details see Table 12 in Battle Orders 17, *US Army Infantry Divisions 1942-43*.

It is not enough for an efficient system of logistics to feed and water the troops, to keep them in ammunition, and to repair their equipment. The logistics system must also use as few resources as possible. It must ensure that supply deliveries are so timely and reliable that the combat troops can enhance their mobility by carrying only minimal supplies with them. It was a new series of purpose-designed military trucks introduced during 1940–42 that revolutionized US Army logistics. The upgraded engines, all-wheel drive, and balloon tires of these new trucks gave them cross-country mobility as good as most animal transportation, and the trucks were built in such numbers that they replaced most animal transport completely. The new trucks could travel much greater distances in much less time than even the trucks they replaced and they enabled the US Army to adopt a new supply system that completely removed divisions and corps from the chain of supply (except in emergencies). Instead, regiments and separate battalions sustained themselves directly from Army-level ammunition and supply distribution points typically set up 20–30 miles to their rear (an hour's drive in good conditions).

An early war Chevrolet G7117 1.5-ton truck with a front-mounted winch photographed at the Ft Holabird Quartermaster Depot, Baltimore, MD on December 10, 1941. Later vehicles had a soft cab. An infantry division was allowed 107 of these trucks (105 by February 1945). An infantry regiment had 30 (31 after February 1944). The rest were split between the division headquarters and signal companies and the medical battalion. This truck had a curb weight of about 8,000 lb. and a gross weight of about 13,000. It could tow 8,000 lb. on a road (half of that cross-country) and carry 15 troops. With the 10,000 lb. front-mounted winch removed, it became a G7107. The Army built nearly 13,000 of both types. For more details see Table 12 in Battle Orders 17, *US Army Infantry Divisions 1942-43*.

Infantry logistics

For the infantry, the new system functioned through the infantry regiment service company. The regimental S-4 (supply) officer belonged to this company but his deputy actually commanded it. Most of the service company was split between a regimental headquarters platoon that did the paperwork, and a transportation platoon that furnished vehicles and drivers.

The regimental headquarters platoon was merely a collective title for the regimental staff and supply sections. The staff section contained the enlisted (and some officer) assistants for the S-1 (personnel) and S-3 (operations) officers. The S-1 assistants were further split between a personnel staff (which, unsurprisingly, attended to personnel administration) and a special service staff (in charge of morale, recreation, postal, and chaplain services). The personnel staff comprised the personnel officer and personnel and "classification" clerks in the staff section. It also directed and supervised the company clerks from all 19 companies in the regiment.

The regimental supply section operated as an office group, a receiving and distributing group, and an ammunition group. The office group maintained records, consolidated requisitions and receipts, and compiled reports. The receiving and distributing group took delivery of all classes of supply except class V (ammunition), established distribution points, and sorted and apportioned the supplies received. Since the group had only a few clerks, working parties furnished by the receiving units did most of the labor. The regimental ammunition officer, ammunition sergeant and a 2¹/₂-ton truck and driver formed the ammunition group. This group supervised the regimental ammunition point and the ammunition vehicles under regimental control. The battalion pioneer platoons supplied labor when needed. The 2¹/₂-ton truck ensured that the group always had at least one vehicle available for short-notice ammunition deliveries.

The transportation platoon itself consisted of a truck section for every battalion and separate company in the regiment. It also had a section that maintained all of the regiment's vehicles. The battalion and company sections included a 2¹/₂-ton truck and trailer for the baggage and field kitchen of every company. Each battalion section also had two trucks carrying an ammunition reserve for the rifle companies. These trucks had no cargo trailers so they would be free to pull water trailers supplied by higher headquarters. The lieutenant and staff sergeant in each battalion truck section became S-4 and supply sergeant, respectively, of the battalion they supported.

A Diamond-T Model 969A 6x6 four-ton wrecker with winch photographed at Ft Holabird Quartermaster Depot, Baltimore, MD on December 10, 1941. The curb weight of this vehicle was 21,350 lb. and it carried a 150,000 lb. winch. More than 6,000 were built. For more details see Table 12 in Battle Orders 17, *US Army Infantry Divisions 1942-43*. An infantry division had only four of these trucks: two with the ordnance maintenance company and one each with the 155mm howitzer and combat engineer battalions. In the division ordnance company there was also a heavier (30,000 lb. curb weight) M1A1 6-ton wrecker.

The maintenance section and the company kitchen and baggage vehicles typically occupied a bivouac area a few miles behind the regiment's frontline. This area was supposed to be beyond the range of enemy light artillery and to offer some cover and concealment during daylight. Here the maintenance section did its work and the company cooks and cook's helpers prepared meals. The meals would be field rations A or B. Both of these were hot meals such as might be served in garrison. A rations needed refrigeration but B rations did not. The objective was to serve two hot meals per day. The third meal was usually field ration C, a canned ration that required no preparation. It could be heated but did not count as a hot meal. Field ration D was an emergency ration consisting of several high-energy chocolate bars. Ideally, breakfast would be a hot meal served just before dawn while dinner would also be hot and served after dark. Darkness allowed the kitchen trucks to approach the frontline without drawing fire.

In April 1945, near Roffeno, Italy a pack mule carries a .50-cal machine gun tripod and three ammunition boxes – a 200 lb. load. The rugged terrain in the Apennines frequently precluded or restricted the use of motor vehicles. Infantry divisions operating there improvised their own pack mule trains in order to get their supplies forward.

The biggest challenge to the supply system was ammunition. Ammunition had to be delivered in great, but essentially unpredictable, quantities and on very short notice. Designated vehicles within the regiment carried an initial load of ammunition calculated to last until a regular flow of ammunition could be established. The weapons carriers in the rifle and weapons companies carried much of this ammunition. In an offensive battle they waited in their "off-carrier" positions to serve as floating ammunition dumps, and they followed their crew-served weapons according to the course of the battle. In the defense, the carriers dropped their ammunition loads at their off-carrier positions (or near command posts) and moved to the rear. Weapon squad ammunition bearers or battalion pioneers would return to these vehicles or dumps to pick up more ammunition for as long as there was any available. When directed by the transport corporals or sergeants the weapons carriers would head for ammunition supply points (ASPs) further back for more ammunition. ASPs existed at all echelons from battalion level up. Sometimes companies established ASPs. An ASP was simply a point at which ammunition was collected for subsequent distribution. It could be moved in accordance with the situation. The battalion pioneer platoons would supply working parties for battalion ASPs (close to the frontline) and the regimental ASP (two or three miles back). They would load empty weapons carriers with whatever ammunition was on hand or send them an army-level ASP by way of the division supply point (usually just a movement control point). Service company trucks were supposed to make the runs to higher-level ASPs but weapons carriers might do so as well. The drivers of all service company trucks not otherwise engaged would get ammunition requisitions and instructions to fill them at the army ASP or wherever they could.

The rear of a GM 2½-ton CCKW 6x6 truck equipped with a "Number 7" wrecker set. This consisted of a frame and pulley for lifting and a front-mounted winch. Though inferior to a purpose-designed wrecker it was adequate for many smaller jobs. This vehicle was photographed at the Holabird Quartermaster Depot, Baltimore, MD on December 10, 1941.

The trucks would constantly shuttle between the different ASPs and the frontline. They had to race to deliver new ammunition before the troops used up their existing supplies. Naturally, shorter distances and better roads made the job much easier. Vehicles could make many more runs during the same amount of time. Nevertheless, for serious combat the service company almost always needed additional trucks from a higher headquarters. The ammunition shuttle would only end when the fighting was over and all units had reconstituted their original ammunition loads.

Artillery logistics

The artillery logistical system worked somewhat differently to that of the infantry. Battalion service batteries were the key to it. The division artillery headquarters only set goals and policies and monitored supply and administrative activities. Every battery had its maintenance section but this section actually included only one or two auto or tractor mechanics (plus aircraft mechanics if the battery had aircraft). It was really a supply section for all supply classes except ammunition. The section also included the cooks and its 2^{1}/$_{2}$-ton truck carried the field kitchen.

Each battalion service battery had two maintenance sections, one for itself and one for the battalion. The battalion section really was a maintenance section, battalion-level supply being (for all items other than ammunition) the job of a separate supply section. However, with only one 2^{1}/$_{2}$-ton truck, the battalion supply section could not carry sufficient gasoline or rations for the battalion's needs. Trucks from the battalion ammunition train sometimes had to assist.

Five "gun sections" constituted the "business end" of a howitzer battery. The first four sections had guns, but instead of a gun the fifth section had two prime movers (with trailers) to carry ammunition and .50-caliber machine guns for antiaircraft defense. The prime movers could be trucks or tractors. The M5 tractor (see *Combat mission and preparation for war*) offered more power and superior off-road performance especially over soft ground, but it needed more fuel and maintenance, was tiring to drive, and hard to control on icy roads. It also did not have adequate space for a crew and ammunition. It was still the preferred prime mover for 155mm howitzers and heavier weapons. Only seven of the Army's 133 155mm howitzer battalions had not converted to tractors by VE day. However, trucks were preferred for 105mm howitzers. Only 51 of 246 towed 105mm battalions (all in the Pacific Theater) used tractors.

Ammunition supply in an artillery battalion was the primary concern of the service battery's ammunition train. Ammunition train trucks made the runs between the howitzer batteries and the ASP. Howitzer battery "fifth sections" often had to make these runs also but in tractor-equipped battalions the limitations of the tractors made this difficult. Tractor-drawn battalions in Europe and the Mediterranean dealt with the problem by "unofficially" replacing one tractor per fifth section with a pair of 4-ton trucks with trailers. The other tractor was kept as a spare.

The ASP allocated artillery ammunition in the form of "credits." A credit was a specified amount of ammunition reserved for a specified unit at a specified ASP for a specified period of time. The credit was usually given so that the artillery could support particular operations within particular time frames. Any ammunition credits not used within the time allotted would revert to the headquarters that had issued them.

This overhead view of a Dodge WC-62 1^{1}/$_{2}$-ton truck shows how this vehicle could stow ammunition when used in a weapons carrier role. The WC-62 (WC-63 when it carried a winch) was really a 6x6 "stretched" version of the WC-51 ^{3}/$_{4}$-ton 4x4 weapons carrier (for details see Table 12 in Battle Orders 17). The curb weight of the WC-62 was 6,925 lb. (or 1,280 lb. heavier than a WC-51; the WC-63's winch added another 325 lb.) and gross vehicle weight was 12,125 lb. The cargo bed was 40 percent larger than that of a WC-51/52 and could seat 12 troops (rather than eight). However, the engine and horsepower rating were the same and this limited these trucks' ability to carry a full-weight load cross-country. The WC-62/63 was often substituted for the WC-51/52 in the tactical maintenance vehicle role because many mechanics regarded the WC-51/52 as too small. The Army built more than 43,000 WC-62/63.

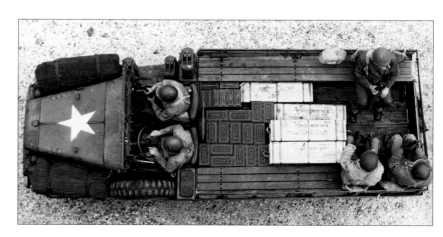

Determining how much 155mm ammunition a given vehicle could carry was fairly easy. Projectiles of this caliber were shipped to combat theaters on pallets, which were broken up prior to issue. Using units needed brackets to prevent the now loose projectiles from rolling about in moving vehicles. The most common type of bracket held 18 projectiles. A 4-ton truck that was towing a howitzer (or a 2½-ton truck that was not) would carry two brackets (36 projectiles). A 4-ton truck that was not towing a howitzer would carry three brackets (54 projectiles) and either it or a 2½-ton truck would also tow a 1-ton or M10 trailer with 18 additional projectiles. An M5 tractor had space for only twenty-four 155mm projectiles. However, it could tow an M21 ammunition trailer loaded with up to 72 projectiles. Unfortunately M21 trailers were only available late in the war. Until then the tractors had to make do with M10 trailers, sometimes drawing two or three of them in tandem. A tractor-equipped howitzer battery also had an extra 2½-ton truck with driver and trailer to carry the personnel and ammunition that its tractors had no room for.

Determining capacity for 105mm ammunition was more difficult. Ammunition of this type was shipped in 100 lb. wooden boxes (two rounds per box) and these were not broken open until just prior to firing. The boxes were stackable and needed no brackets to keep them in place. Thus, the capacity for 105mm ammunition of a given truck or trailer would be determined by how much space it had and how much weight it could bear.

At the beginning of any major operation it was common to stage ammunition in the firing batteries' initial positions in excess of what the firing batteries and ammunition trains could carry. A battery would use up its staged ammunition first so that it could move to its next firing position with a full ammunition load. If a battery could not use all its staged ammunition prior to moving it would abandon what was left and report its location to higher headquarters.

A jeep with trailer photographed in 1942. After June 1943 an infantry division was allowed 637 jeeps and 278 trailers. By February 1945 this had increased to 665 jeeps and 317 trailers. The curb weight of a jeep was 2,450 lb. The Army built more than 600,000 of them (and more than 140,000 trailers). For more details see Table 12 in Battle Orders 17, *US Army Infantry Divisions 1942-43.*

A late-model 2½-ton CCKW-353 truck of the 351st Ordnance Battalion photographed at the dispersal area of Chabua Airfield, Assam Province, India on December 1, 1944. The CCKW weighed 11,000 lb. curb weight (16,000 lb. gross). It could carry 10,000 lb. on a road or 5,000 cross-country or up to 25 troops. There was an optional 10,000 lb. winch. The Army built more than 412,000 of them. Dump truck, air compressor and shop van versions existed as well. In July 1943 an infantry division rated 269 of the standard CCKW-353, 84 of the short wheel based CCKW-352, 27 dump trucks and three shop vans. By January 1945 there were 10 more CCKW-353 and three fewer CCKW-352. For more details see Table 12 in Battle Orders 17, *US Army Infantry Divisions 1942-43.*

American wounded receive treatment at a hastily established aid station in the square at Troyes, France, August 26, 1944.

Medical treatment and evacuation

The US Army organized its medical system around the need to get wounded soldiers off the battlefield as soon as possible and into the hands of trained medical orderlies. The wounded soldier would pass through a chain of stations, each able to provide more extensive care than the last. The chain ended in a general hospital. However only the most seriously wounded needed to go that far. Most men could recover at some lower station and eventually return to duty. The lowest level of the chain was the medical aidman ("medic") who usually ranked as a T-4 or T-5 surgical technician. The medical detachment of an infantry regiment would attach a medic to every rifle, machine-gun, or mortar platoon in the regiment. This medic would administer first aid to and arrange the evacuation of as many wounded as he could. He would direct "walking wounded" to the battalion aid station or have litter teams carry the "non-walking." The aid station provided only the minimum treatment necessary to save life or limb or to patch a man up so he could return to his unit. If a patient still needed care he could be evacuated to the regimental aid station, which had somewhat better facilities or he could go to one of the two clearing stations in the division medical battalion's clearing company. Each was essentially a small field hospital able to care for a limited number of patients for a limited time. Patients needing further treatment or who were in excess of clearing station capacity could be sent on to more capable corps- and army-level hospitals further to the rear.

One collecting company per medical battalion was normally associated with each infantry regiment in the division. It transported wounded from the battalion aid stations to the regimental station and the clearing stations. The preferred method of moving a patient was by ambulance but the company had a litter platoon (10 four-man litter teams) to collect casualties from places that an ambulance could not reach. The litter platoon could also reinforce battalion litter teams. Each litter team included a medic who could keep the patient alive until he reached his destination. Each collecting company also had a small station platoon that was intended to serve as an intermediate aid station between the battalion and regimental aid stations and the clearing stations. However, since intermediate stations were seldom needed the station platoons usually just reinforced the clearing stations.

Quartermaster, ordnance, and engineer logistical functions

Although the infantry division in the US Army had ceased to be a normal link in the chain of supply by 1940, it retained certain assets that allowed it to intervene in logistical emergencies and reduce its dependence on non-divisional service units. The US Army Quartermaster Corps had (and still has) many service support functions but for the infantry division it mainly provided motor transport. An infantry division quartermaster company had the same complement of trucks as a standard quartermaster truck company. These trucks all carried standard "organic" supply loads that could be issued at the discretion of the division commander. In this way they acted as a kind of "floating" supply reserve. If the trucks were needed for other purposes, they could make themselves available by dropping their organic loads (with the help of the service platoon). The service platoon not only performed labor duties itself but, alternatively, it could also supervise civilian or prisoner of war labor. Army-level supply and ammunition points supplied the labor needed to load any division trucks that were sent there.

The organic trucks of an infantry division only sufficed to meet its supply requirements in a quiet sector or rear area. For serious combat higher headquarters would provide additional truck companies. These would work through the division quartermaster officer. In Europe a division in combat would usually have three companies attached to it, but if it wanted to move all its infantry by truck in one lift it would need six companies. Inasmuch as so many companies were seldom available most divisions executing a rapid movement improvised by piling troops on the tanks and self-propelled guns normally attached to them or by having their trucks make several trips. In this way, a US infantry division could make itself as mobile as a Panzer division.

The division's ordnance light maintenance company reduced its dependency on corps- and army-level repair shops for third-echelon maintenance. First-echelon maintenance was driver maintenance. Second-echelon was that performed by the mechanics belonging to using units such as an infantry regimental service company or an artillery battalion or battery maintenance section. Ordnance personnel performed third echelon maintenance when working in the field or fourth echelon maintenance when working in a permanent depot. One light maintenance company was not nearly enough to meet the needs of a division in combat but McNair wanted to centralize most maintenance above the division level to save skilled manpower. Instead of enlarging the division maintenance company or adding another, McNair persuaded the War Department to authorize second-echelon mechanics to perform all the third-echelon jobs that their time, skills, and tools would allow. Of the rest, the lengthy repair jobs would go to depots or higher-level maintenance companies. The division maintenance company would focus its efforts on jobs that required special tools, expertise, or both, but did not call for much time.

Division commanders were not at all pleased with this arrangement. Their light maintenance companies could only perform about one-third of the repair jobs sent to them. Most divisions contrived to get a second light or a medium maintenance company more or less permanently attached to them, so they could perform more of the repairs they needed "in house."

The engineers had only limited logistical functions. The most important of these was that of ensuring the supply of potable water to the division. The engineer battalion service section had four water supply units, each transported by a $2^1/_2$-ton truck. Three of the units, each with a four-man crew, established a water point for each infantry regiment (and supporting elements). The fourth unit was a spare.

The Corps of Engineers furnished maps and tools such as compasses, surveying instruments, and slide rules. It also supplied class IV supplies such as fortification material, paint (except ordnance paint), and nails. The division engineer battalion got involved with this distribution only if locally acquired or captured maps or class IV materials were available. In this case the battalion would establish supply points for these items and supervise their distribution.

Combat operations

This chapter briefly describes three 1944–45 campaigns involving US Army infantry divisions.

1st Infantry Division (Reinforced), Omaha Beach, June 6, 1944

Ever since the defeat of the British and French armies at the hands of the Germans in 1940, British Prime Minister Winston Churchill and, later, US President Franklin Roosevelt had planned to land another Allied army in France. This army would open a "second front" to draw German forces away from the Soviet Union, liberate France, and enable an Allied invasion of Germany from the west. The Allies chose to land in Normandy rather than the more favorably situated Pas de Calais area to the northeast because the Normandy defenses were much weaker.

Taking advantage of their air and naval supremacy Allies would spearhead their assault with five reinforced infantry divisions. In the west the US 4th Division would land on "Utah" Beach, on the southeast coast of the Cotentin Peninsula. Moving eastward, the US 1st Division and part of the 29th would land at "Omaha" Beach; the British 50th Division would land on "Gold;" the Canadian 3rd Division on "Juno"; and the British 3rd Division on "Sword."

Although the Allies were mostly unopposed at sea and in the air and would enjoy a comfortable superiority in numbers and firepower on the ground, they were concerned about the success of their beach landings. Any landing would essentially be a frontal assault against a fortified position that stood little chance of achieving surprise. "Saturating" the beaches with rockets, naval gunfire, and air strikes could help but darkness or smoke would likely hamper the attackers as much as the defenders. Also, the Allies would be moving their troops ashore in lightly armed and armored landing craft. Rifle and weapons companies in the initial waves would get special training and be reorganized into 30-man sections that would each fit in a standard landing craft. These units would resume their normal organization as soon as they could get off the beach.

Tanks would closely follow the assault waves. Some of these would come ashore in landing craft. Others would float ashore by erecting a large canvas "bloomer" to increase their volume to where they could float by displacement. Twin screws or "duplex drive" powered by the tanks' engines would provide propulsion. Tanks so equipped were known as "DD" tanks.

Two Americans advance cautiously toward the bodies of recently killed Germans near St. Lo, France, July 31, 1944.

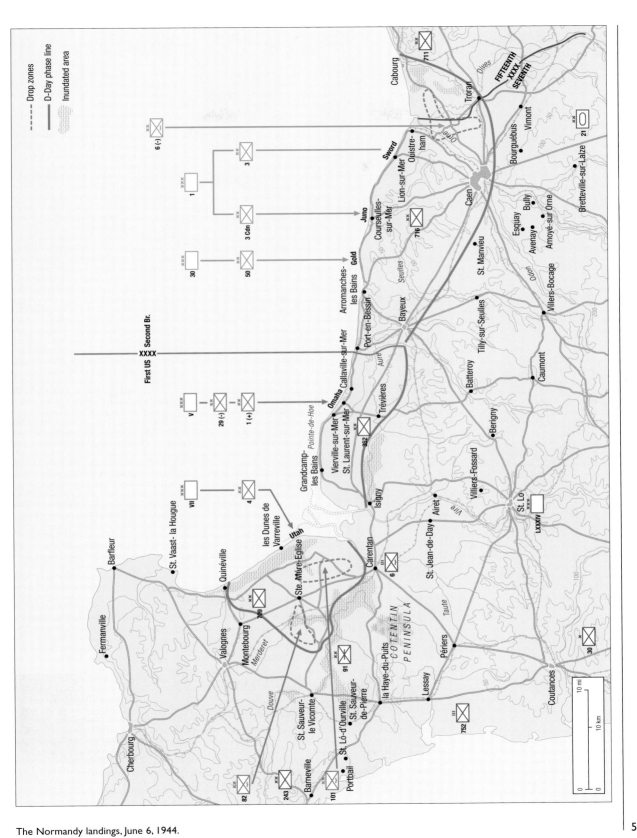

The Normandy landings, June 6, 1944.

A bulldozer smoothes out a bomb crater during the opening of Operation *Cobra* (Normandy, August 5, 1944). Note the wrecked jeep in the foreground. This appears to be part of the bomb damage accidentally inflicted by Army Air Corps aircraft as *Cobra* began. The D7 tractor with angle-dozer was the standard bulldozer in division combat engineer battalions; updated versions of it are still in use today.

By mid-1944 the German Wehrmacht was no longer the victorious military machine of three years earlier. Disasters in Russia and the strains of prolonged war and economic blockade were pushing the German population and economy towards breaking point. Nearly everything was in short supply and the Russian front had priority for whatever was available.

The divisions defending the coast were almost entirely infantry. To make better use of their limited resources and because they had raised many more divisions than they could sustain, the Germans in late 1943 began converting their infantry divisions from the "1941 Type" of about 17,200 men each to the "1944 Type" of about 13,000. They hoped that larger numbers of automatic weapons and mortars would balance the loss in manpower. They also hoped that bazookas copied from captured US weapons (but in a larger caliber) plus Panzerfaust rocket-propelled antitank grenades and plenty of courage would compensate for shortages in antitank guns. There were no major changes in the division artillery. However, an infantry regiment in a 1944 division would have only two battalions rather than three (as in 1941). To partly offset this, a 1944 division would also have a "Fusilier" battalion, organized just like an infantry battalion but with extra bicycles for mobility. It would act as a reserve or reconnaissance unit.

The bulk of the German infantry divisions in France were "static" (*bodenständig*) divisions. Recruited from older men in their mid thirties, static divisions had only just enough transport to maintain themselves in a fixed position. They needed additional vehicles to move anywhere. Organizationally, they differed from standard infantry divisions in that they were each supposed to have two three-battalion infantry regiments rather than three two-battalion regiments. In lieu of a weapons company, a static infantry battalion was supposed to distribute its crew-served weapons more or less evenly among its four rifle companies. In practice, however, static divisions seldom conformed to official tables and it was hard to find two of them alike.

To augment their static divisions the Germans used large numbers of ex-Soviet prisoners of war. These men had signed up in order to fight Communism and to eat three meals a day, but they had little interest in fighting the Western Allies. Field Marshal Gerd von Rundstedt, who commanded all the German armies in France, Belgium, and Holland, thought them dangerously unreliable. These "volunteers" formed a series of Ost or "Eastern" battalions, some of which operated independently and others as integral parts of German (static) infantry regiments. They mainly used captured Soviet weapons.

The majority of the Panzer or Panzer Grenadier divisions in France were there to recuperate from the Russian front. At the beginning of June 1944 most were re-equipping themselves and integrating new recruits. They had only a fraction of their authorized vehicles because they were not expected to need much mobility in France. British and American postwar historians have often credited the slow German response to the Normandy landings to Hitler sleeping late and to the success of Allied deception measures. In fact, the biggest reason was the lack of trucks. Field Marshal Irwin Rommel, commanding Army Group G tasked with defending the coast from Brittany to Holland, believed that, given Allied air supremacy, an armored counterattack would have been useless in any case. He had pressed for beach defenses that could defeat the invasion at the water's edge but there were not nearly enough Germans in Normandy to do this.

Most of the German troops in Normandy belonged to the LXXXIV Corps, which was under the Seventh Army and Army Group G. One of its seven divisions, the newly reformed 21st Panzer, was stationed generally south and east of Caen as the primary counterattack force. The rest of the divisions were infantry. Of these, the 319th garrisoned the Channel Islands and was therefore effectively out of the picture. The 243rd (plus a collection of Ost battalions under the 752nd Regimental Headquarters) held the west coast of the Cotentin Peninsula, while the 709th, a static division with eight German and three Ost battalions, held the east coast, including Utah Beach. The 716th Infantry Division, another static division with six German and three Ost battalions, held all the beaches (including Omaha, Gold, Juno, and Sword) from Carentan to the Orne estuary. In reserve in and just south of the Cotentin Peninsula were the weak (7,000–8,000-man) 91st Air Landing Division, the 6th Parachute Regiment, the three-battalion 30th "Mobile" (actually, bicycle) Brigade, and smaller units. On D-Day most of them opposed the US airborne landings. It was obvious that the 716th Division with its 10,000 or so middle-aged reservists and Soviet POWs had far too large a sector. Therefore in March 1944 the LXXXIV Corps ordered a new infantry division, the 352nd to take over the 716th Division sector between Carentan and Le Homel (near to the middle of Gold Beach). Activated at St. Lo in November 1943, the 10,000-man 352nd Division (seven German and no Ost battalions) was recruited from relatively bright and eager 17- and 18-year-olds, but shortages of fuel and ammunition and the need to build beach defenses greatly interfered with their training.

When the 352nd Division assumed its new sector, the 716th Division left its 726th Regiment with two German and one Ost battalions in their original positions under 352nd Division control. The resultant intermingling and cross attachment of units, together with subsequent losses of German records, have made it difficult to know exactly who was where. However, it is known that the 914th Infantry, 352nd Division, had the sector running from Carentan to a point about midway between Isigny and Pointe-de-Hoe

US troops are shown marching down the street in Dornot, France, as they advance on the Moselle River, September 8, 1944. A jeep and trailer are on the right.

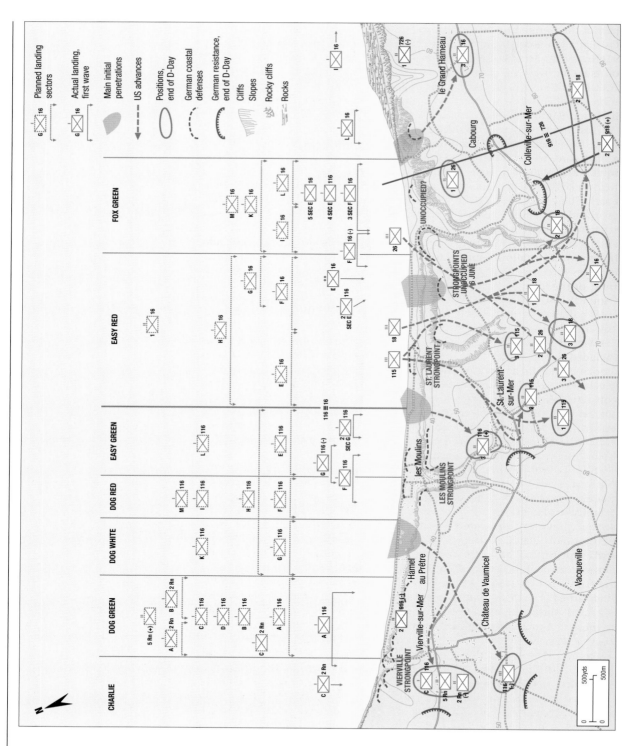

The infantry assaults on Omaha Beach, June 6, 1944.

(a.k.a. Pointe du Hoc). From there the 916th Infantry sector ran to the village of Colleville-sur-Mer on the eastern half of Omaha Beach. The 726th Infantry took over from there to the end of the 352nd Division sector at Le Homel. The 915th Infantry and 352nd Fusilier battalion (both of the 352nd Division) were in LXXXIV Corps reserve near Bayeux. The 726th Infantry had left its 3rd Battalion in the Grandcamp area west of Pointe-de-Hoe, a less threatened part of the German line under the 916th Regiment's control. It left its 439th Ost Battalion around Isigny, an even less threatened area. In exchange, the 916th gave its 1st Battalion to the 726th, which placed it in the western half of its sector, which included part of Gold Beach. This left the 1st Battalion, 726th Infantry holding the eastern third of the Omaha Beach and probably some of the coast to the west towards Pointe-de-Hoe, while the 2nd Battalion/916th was supposed to hold the rest.

This meant that probably fewer than 1,000 Germans defended Omaha when the Americans came ashore. Since a continuous defensive line for such a small force was impossible the Germans deployed their troops in a series of squad- and platoon-sized "resistance nests." These could be strung together to form larger strong points. The strong points were on average about 1,200m apart. There was no depth to the defense at all and most positions lacked overhead cover. This writer has visited Omaha Beach and it is a fairly level stretch of sand, no more than a few hundred yards deep at low tide and ending in a line of high bluffs through which run several draws that could be improved to allow vehicles to exit the beach. The Germans sited their defenses to cover these draws. They built three main strong points. One in front of the village of Vierville-sur-Mer included a well-sited bunker with a 75mm Pak 40 antitank gun (sometimes erroneously described as an 88mm) able to deliver flanking fire across most of the beach. The gun is still there. Towards the center of the beach and covering the draws running through Les Moulins and in front of St. Laurent-sur-Mer was another complex that included a 75mm Pak 97/38, an improvisation consisting of a captured French 75mm field gun mounted on a 50mm Pak 38 antitank gun carriage. Much less powerful than a Pak 40 it was emplaced in a small complex of concrete shelters just off the beach. On the eastern end of the beach and sited for flanking fire are three concrete shelters (platforms with concrete roofs, not real pillboxes), probably occupied on D-Day by the three 50mm antitank guns belonging to the 726th Infantry. These shelters still bear 75mm shot holes from the American tanks that made it ashore.

The US 1st Infantry Division's landing on Omaha began to go wrong from the start. The attached 116th Infantry with the 2nd and 5th Ranger battalions was supposed to land on the right (west) half of the beach while the 16th Infantry landed on the left (east side). Part of the Rangers would capture the 155mm gun battery at Pointe-de-Hoe so it could not threaten the left flank of the assault. Because of concern about hitting friendly troops, most of the air strikes hit behind the German positions rather than in them. The seas were almost too rough for the landing, and sank most of the DD tanks that tried to get ashore as well as most of the landing boats and DUKW amphibious trucks that carried the artillery. Mist, dust, and smoke from the naval bombardment obscured landmarks and a two- to three-knot current carried many units well to the east of their intended landing points. Heavy enemy fire tended to isolate boat sections even when they were only a few hundred yards apart. This made assembly and reorganization impossible. On the west side Company A, 116th Infantry and Company C of the 2nd Ranger Battalion actually came ashore where they were supposed to, but fire from the Vierville strong point killed or wounded two-thirds of Company A and half the Rangers before they could shelter in the relative safety of the sea wall at the base of the cliff. The current had carried the two companies that were supposed to land to the left of Company A 1,000 yards too far east. Further to the east a third of the 2nd/116 landing in the 16th Infantry zone just east of Les Moulins were sufficiently screened by smoke and fire that German fire directed against them was sporadic and ineffective. The 16th Infantry also found a soft spot. Four boat sections landing between St. Laurent and Colleville were able to cross the beach with only two casualties, though other units nearby suffered heavily. Some of the German resistance nests atop the bluffs in this sector turned out to have been unoccupied. Another positive development was that the 116th Infantry concluded that the sea was too rough for DD tanks and sent its 32 attached tanks ashore in landing craft. Twenty-four of them landed successfully.

The heavy losses and disorganization experienced by the initial assault waves naturally impacted on the follow-on waves. German fire prevented the engineers from blowing gaps in the beach obstacles set up to hole and sink landing craft proceeding to the beach. At low water most of these were exposed but the tide was coming in and these obstacles could soon become a serious threat. Follow-on waves that reached the beach only added to the crowding and confusion that reigned there. In the east the rest of 2nd/116th and another Ranger company landed in front of Vierville to reinforce the remains of A Company, but the newcomers were also shot to pieces except for Company C, which fortunately landed by accident 1,000 yards too far east. But still further to the east the 2nd/116th was faring badly. Losses were lighter in the 16th Infantry sector but the confusion and intermingling of units on the beach was serious. To the Germans it appeared that their defense would succeed. They therefore sent their reserves to shore up the collapsing 716th Division to the east and did not reinforce Omaha.

However the German defense at Omaha was already starting to crack. Intense naval gunfire was having an effect and small groups of Americans found they could infiltrate into and through the thin and porous German defenses. There were four main penetrations, two in each regimental zone. Company C 116th Infantry and 5th Ranger Battalion managed to climb the bluffs just west of Les Moulins, found them unoccupied and then pushed on until they received fire from the flank. The 3rd/116th also found a hole just east of Les Moulins and pushed through it towards the village of St. Laurent. The 16th Infantry pushed through the generally unoccupied bluffs east of St. Laurent. The Germans had fortified this area, but the reinforcements that were to occupy it had never arrived. However, lacking motor vehicles to bring up supplies and heavy weapons the Americans could not exploit their successes, even though they were now in the German rear. However part of G Company, 16th Infantry managed to capture most of the strong point in the St. Laurent exit (by attacking it from behind after the position had taken some naval gunfire hits). This finally opened up an exit that motor vehicles could use. At about the same time an attempt by about 600 men from the 116th Infantry and the Rangers to capture the Vierville redoubt from behind failed, but the Americans did occupy Vierville itself.

The Germans did have local reserves operating behind their main line of resistance (MLR) – mainly artillerymen, engineers, and support troops – and they managed to limit American penetrations and hold onto St. Laurent. However, a counterattack in the east by the 2nd Battalion, 915th Infantry (released from LXXXIV Corps reserve) accomplished little beyond securing Colleville. By evening the 115th Infantry (part of V Corps floating reserve) and the 18th and 26th Infantry (1st Division) had landed. The 352nd Division could only respond with its last reserve, its engineer battalion. The 30th Mobile Brigade arrived next day but it was not enough. With the collapse of the 716th Division at Gold, Juno, and Sword and American infiltration behind Omaha the German position became untenable. The 352nd Division pulled back to an assembly area southeast of Isigny. Their attempts to trap the surviving Germans in their beach defenses largely failed but the Americans had achieved their key objectives for the Omaha landing. The other four landings had gone smoothly against much less opposition. The V Corps initially reported its losses for June 6 as 2,374 killed, wounded, and missing. Subsequent "corrections" reduced this figure as stragglers and missing men turned up, but the actual losses would not have been fewer than 2,000.

The chief of staff of the 352nd Division later estimated that on June 6 his division had lost 200 killed in action, 500 wounded, and 500 missing (mainly captured) but these would have included losses sustained at Gold Beach, Pont-de-Hoe, and in an ill-fated counterattack on Gold and Juno.

The Allies were firmly established ashore and able to begin the next stage of their campaign.

28th Infantry Division in the Ardennes, December 16–19, 1944

By the autumn of 1944, it seemed like the final defeat of Germany, at the hands of the Soviet Union and the Western Allied powers was near. After their breakout from Normandy the Allies had raced across France, driving the German occupation forces out of most of that country, and had seized parts of Germany. At the same time Germany was suffering major disasters in the east. General Dwight D. Eisenhower, commanding the Allied forces, had bet Field Marshal Bernard L. Montgomery, commanding the British Commonwealth forces, that the war would be over by Christmas.

On paper at least the Wehrmacht still had 8.4 million men (including 700,000 sick and wounded) under arms as of December 1944 and the German economy could still clothe, feed, water, and arm them. However, German military manpower was still in critically short supply and the quality of new recruits was well below that of only six months before.

However, the war was not quite over yet. The Allies, after their post-Normandy race across France, had outrun their supplies. The Germans exploited this vulnerability with a series of counterattacks that drove the Allies out of most of the German territory they had occupied.

On September 16, 1944, Hitler reacted to this relatively good news by ordering a major offensive through the Ardennes forests to capture Antwerp, Belgium's main seaport and a major link in the Allied supply chain. A similar maneuver in 1940 had led to the fall of France. A repeat in 1944 could gain for Germany (Hitler believed) a negotiated peace with the Western Allies. Unfortunately, the necessary conditions for success were lacking. In 1940, a far more capable German army enjoyed good weather, a superior air force, and adequate supplies. In 1944 the Germans would attack in winter over muddy and icy roads with inadequate supplies and a greatly outnumbered air force. The Ardennes forests, rugged terrain, and sparse road network strongly favored any defender. Even in 1940, to send a mechanized army through it was risky. In 1944, as Hitler's generals tried to tell him, it was foolhardy. It was true that the Germans would start their offensive with an overall local numerical

US infantrymen cross the Winterspelter River near the German border, using the broken fragments of a bridge, September 12, 1944.

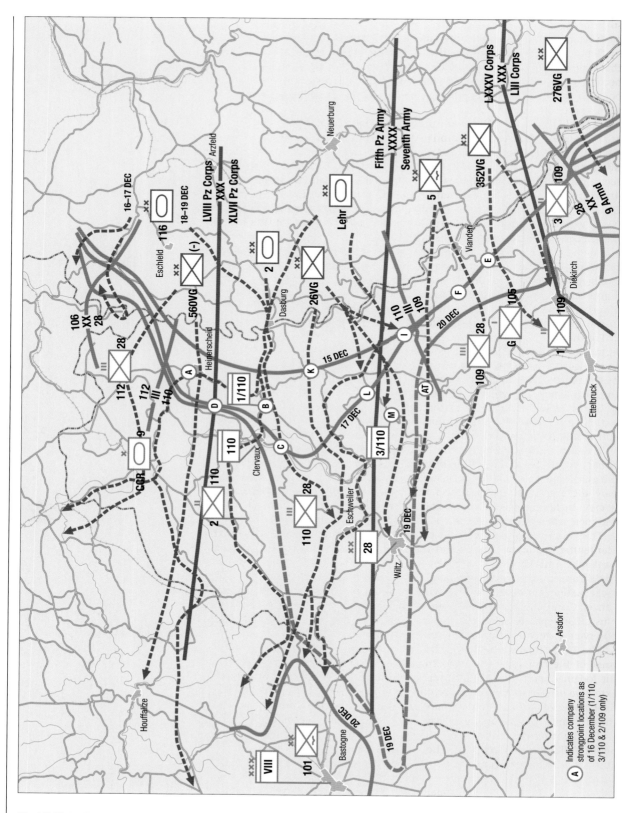

The US 28th Infantry Division sector in the Battle of the Bulge.

superiority of 2½ to 1 (5 to 1 in the 28th Division's sector) but in 1940 it had been nearer 15 to 1. Furthermore, unlike the Belgians in 1940, the Americans in 1944 could and did reinforce their troops in the Ardennes very quickly, so that the initial German numerical superiority on the ground would soon become an inferiority. However, Hitler needed a successful offensive and he believed that the odds of executing one against the Soviets were even worse than against the Americans.

The bulk of the US forces that initially faced the German attack were under Major General Troy H. Middleton's VIII Corps, part of Lieutenant General Courtney H. Hodges' First US Army. As of December 15, 1944, General Middleton had placed his 106th Infantry Division in the northern part of his sector, Major General Norman Cota's 28th Division in the center and the 4th Infantry Division and Combat Command (brigade) A of the 9th Armored Division in the south. The 9th Armored Division's reserve combat command (CCR) was moving north to V Corps. Its combat command (brigade) "B" (CCB) had already reached the V Corps sector. In all, the VIII Corps' 69,000 officers and men held a front of about 85 miles, or about three times what US doctrine recommended. General Hodges was aware of the risks but he urgently needed troops elsewhere. The 106th Division had only just arrived from the United States but the 4th and 28th divisions were veteran units. Both had recently absorbed some 9,000 trained but inexperienced replacements to make good the losses they had sustained during their recent drive to the Roer River.

For their offensive the Germans placed the Sixth Panzer Army in the north, facing the 99th Division (V Corps) and the 14th Cavalry Group. In the center they placed General Hasso von Manteuffel's Fifth Panzer Army, facing the 28th and 106th divisions. The Seventh Army, an all-infantry force, protected the Fifth Panzer Army's left (southern) flank.

In the Fifth Panzer Army sector the LXVI Corps (two infantry divisions) initially opposed the 106th Division. The LVIII and XLVII Panzer Corps faced the 28th Division further south.

The 28th Division occupied by far the largest sector in the US VIII Corps. General Cota had to put all three of his infantry regiments in his frontline facing the Our River (the boundary between Germany and Luxembourg). He retained only the 2nd/110th Infantry and the attached 707th Tank Battalion as his reserve. Including attachments his division mustered only about 17,000 officers and men rather than the 20,000 to 25,000 normal for a US division in combat.

The German offensive did not commence with a great bang. General von Manteuffel had argued for a short preliminary bombardment that would not "wake the Americans" too soon. On paper, the German artillery was strong, the XLVII Panzer Corps having six battalions of cannon artillery and six of multiple rocket launchers in addition to what was organic to its divisions. The LVIII Panzer Corps had five cannon and two multiple rocket-launcher battalions plus a few separate batteries. However, shortages of ammunition and trained observers greatly undermined German artillery effectiveness.

The 112th Infantry in the north held a six-mile wide lodgment on the east bank of the Our River. Its 1st/112th Battalion occupied the northern part of the lodgment and the 3rd/112th was in the south. Field fortifications backed by extensive patches of barbed wire protected both battalions. The 2nd/112th was in reserve west of the Our but it regularly patrolled and manned observation posts on the east bank. For the past several days the 112th Infantry's sector had been quiet.

The fighting element of the LVIII Panzer Corps was the 116th Panzer and 560th Volksgrenadier divisions. The 116th Panzer had recently rebuilt itself by absorbing air force personnel and the separate 108th Panzer Brigade. Though authorized 180 tanks on December 16 it actually had only 41 Panther and 21 Panzer IV tanks, though additional tanks and 14 assault guns were en route. The 116th Panzer was also missing about 40 percent of its trucks, which meant that much of its infantry (four battalions) would have to walk.

Men of the 1st Platoon, Company D, 39th Infantry support a successful attack on the town of Schlich, Germany with a water-cooled .30-cal M1917A1 heavy machine gun, December 10, 1944. Company D was the weapons company for the 1st Battalion. The M1917A1 weighed 41 lb. empty (filling the water jacket would add another 7 lb.) but its tripod, designed to support accurate fire at long range, weighed 53 lb. The gun's water-cooling enabled it to maintain a high rate of fire, as the numerous empty ammunition boxes around this weapon attest.

By this stage of the war most German infantry divisions had been re-organized as Volksgrenadier (VG or "people's infantry") divisions. These were 1,500 men smaller than the 1944 Type that had fought in Normandy, and had only a Fusilier company instead of a battalion. Most VG divisions suffered from too little training, too few veterans, and too few vehicles and antitank guns. Their meager capabilities suited them for little more than defensive combat. Activated only a few months earlier from inexperienced garrison units in Norway and Denmark, the 560th VG was, as of December 16, still 1,400 men under strength, and one of its three regiments was still en route from Denmark. It would start its offensive with only four small infantry battalions and three battalions of artillery. Its initial objective was to capture two bridges over the Our to allow the 116th Panzer to get its tanks across and hopefully isolate the Americans on the east bank. Although some American units were surprised, the inexperienced Volksgrenadiers failed in their initial attacks and sustained significant losses. They did seize a blown bridge further south near the boundary between the 110th and 112th Infantry but a new bridge could not be in place in less than 24 hours.

The 116th Panzer Division initially directed its efforts against the bridges at Burg Reuland in the 106th Division sector and against Oberhausen (behind the 1st/112th Infantry positions). The results were disappointing, though some Germans infiltrated to within sight of Oberhausen. The 116th redirected its attack to the southeast against Oren and, breaking through the seam between 1st/110th and 3rd/110th, managed (with some help from the 560th) to capture the bridge and the town despite strong resistance from the 112th Cannon Company. However, the bridge turned out to be too light to support tanks so the 116th changed direction again and headed south to Dasburg where XLVII Panzer Corps had erected a bridge. It crossed the bridge and turned north. Its reconnaissance battalion (which went first) together with elements of the 560th VG took Heinerscheid from Company A of 1st/110th and threatened the 112th Infantry's left flank. By that time the 112th was withdrawing to the northwest. Its two battalions east of the Our escaped encirclement. Their orders to withdraw had arrived only just in time. Though relatively intact the 112th was soon pushed out of the 28th Division sector. It then came under the control of the 106th Division and participated in the defense of St. Vith. The 116th Panzer assembled itself at Heinerscheid next day and began moving towards Houffalize, which it captured without resistance on the 19th. The 560th VG pressed the 112th Infantry northward and prepared to follow the 116th to the west.

Further to the south, the weakened 110th Infantry was attempting to cover a 9–10-mile front. With its second battalion detached to the division reserve there was no chance of maintaining a continuous line. His situation being similar to what the Germans had faced at Omaha, the regimental commander, Colonel William Fuller, established a system of fortified villages with a rifle or weapons company in each. Patrols, outposts, and observation posts only operated during the day because there was no one to take over after dark. In the 110th sector four roads ran from the German border at the Our uphill to the main north–south highway (which the Americans called "Skyline Drive") and then down again to the Clerf River. The 110th's strong points were sited to block these four roads. The northernmost of the roads was the only one with an all-weather surface. It ran through the town of Clerf (or Clervaux) where the 110th had its headquarters and on to Bastogne, the initial German objective.

Facing the 110th was the XLVII Panzer Corps with the 2nd Panzer Division, Panzer Division Lehr, and the 26th Volksgrenadier Division. The two Panzer divisions had both fought in Normandy but had since been rebuilt. However, Panzer Lehr had recently sustained substantial losses in an offensive against the US Third Army on the Saar. Its infantry battalions were short of riflemen and its tank regiment down to only 54 Panzer IV and Panthers. A brigade of 40 assault guns reinforced it shortly before the offensive began. The 2nd Panzer Division was in better shape with 64 Panthers, 28 Panzer IV, and 24 assault guns in its Panzer Regiment. However, it was at least 300 trucks short. One of its infantry battalions had only bicycles. The 26th VG was an older division rebuilt in September 1944 with navy and air force personnel. Unlike the 560th it had had enough time to whip its new men into reasonable shape. It was also a little stronger than a normal VG division in that it still retained its Fusilier battalion.

The Germans planned to move infantry across the Our in rubber boats the night before the artillery bombardment began. These would secure crossing points over the Our and infiltrate through American lines to seize additional crossing points over the river. Engineers would then erect a heavy bridge at Dasburg for the 2nd Panzer and part of Panzer Lehr (including its tanks). The 26th VG and the rest of Panzer Lehr would use a lighter bridge near Gemünd.

The German offensive fell behind schedule almost immediately when their inexperienced engineers failed to erect the two bridges before nightfall on the 16th. Until the bridges were in place the German infantry's attempts to reduce the fortified American towns were in large measure frustrated because they could not bring up their heavy weapons. This also enabled several platoon-sized counterattacks by the 707th Tank Battalion to achieve some success.

After the Germans began to get their heavy weapons across the Our, the American-held towns began to fall. First to go was Marnach (held by B Company and the headquarters company of 1st/110th and a tank destroyer platoon) during the night of December 16–17. General Cota tried to recover the town the next morning with an attack from the north by the 2nd/110th Infantry, but this failed completely. Two medium tank platoons and Company "C" of 1st/110th then attacked Marnach from Munshausen. The tanks actually reached Marnach only to find no Americans present. They fell back soon afterwards, one tank platoon being ordered to Clerf to strengthen its defenses.

Lead elements of the 2nd Panzer reached Clerf in the late evening of December 16. The headquarters company of the 110th Infantry, various stragglers and small units, including elements of the 707th Tank Battalion and the 9th Armored Division, defended Clerf but organized resistance ceased by the evening of December 17. A group from the headquarters company held out in the chateau until early the next morning. Colonel Fuller was captured along with a small party that he was attempting to lead to safety.

By December 18 the 110th Infantry and the 109th Field Artillery were essentially wiped out. In the north, survivors collected at Donnange to make a stand with Company G and elements of the 9th Armored Division CCR. The survivors of Company C, the 110th Cannon Company, and a section of tank destroyers had abandoned Munshausen.

To the south it was much the same. The Americans abandoned Holzthum (Company L) and Weiler (Company I), and small groups of them escaped westward. Hosingen (Company K and some engineers) surrendered on February 18. The survivors of 3rd/110th defended Consthum for a time and then withdrew to Wiltz. Lieutenant Colonel Daniel

In a wood outside Poffendorf, Germany, across the Erft Canal are two First Army soldiers with an M1919A4 air-cooled .30-cal light machine gun and a BAR, March 2, 1945. The M1919A4 sacrificed long range and sustained rate of fire for less weight. The gun itself weighed 31 lb. and its tripod 14 lb. Like the M1917A1 it was belt fed. The tripod precluded the M1919A4 from being used in an assault. The M1918A2 BAR was the standard squad automatic weapon. It weighed 21 lb. and fired from a 20-round magazine.

Strickler, executive officer of the 110th, took charge of defending Wiltz. He had about 200 survivors from 3rd/110th plus the 44th Combat Engineer Battalion and elements of the 707th Tank, 630th Tank Destroyer, and 687th (separate) Field Artillery battalions. The German attack began in earnest on December 19. The defensive perimeter was soon pierced and the defenders began to run low on ammunition. That evening Strickler decided to evacuate the town. Some of the survivors reached Bastogne on December 20. Others, including Strickler himself, reached Vaux-les-Rosieres.

On the right of the 110th Infantry, the 109th Infantry (and the 107th and 108th Field Artillery) held the southern nine miles of the 28th Division's sector. The 2nd/109th held the northern five miles of this sector with only two company-sized strong points and a reserve at Brandenburg. The 3rd/109th held the southern four miles, but placed most of its forces in a 3,000-yard-long defense line in the triangle formed by the intersection of the Sauer and Our rivers. The 1st/109th was in reserve at Diekrich. Facing the 109th were the 5th Parachute and the 352nd VG divisions belonging to the LXXXV Corps of the German Seventh Army. Originally an elite unit the 5th Parachute now consisted of untrained air force ground crewmen with only a small veteran cadre. The 352nd (the same division that had fought at Normandy) had a stronger cadre to lead its mainly navy and air force recruits, but it was also ill trained and lightly armed and it had orders to avoid direct combat as much as it could.

The German plan was for the 5th Parachute Division's 14th Regiment to cross the Our at Stolzembourg and seize a crossing point on the Wiltz River west of Hoscheid. The 15th would cross the Our at Vianden, seizing the high ground and then a bridgehead over the Sure at Bourscheid. The 13th, which had no trucks, would cross the Our at Roth and mop up the pockets of resistance left by the 14th and 15th. The 352nd VG would cross the Our near Gentingen, seize the heights in the Sauer–Our triangle and push on to Ettelbruck – all on the first day!

After the offensive began, the 14th and 15th regiments easily passed through the 2nd/109th outpost line. The 14th then advanced along the southern flank of the XLVII Panzer Corps until it reached Hoscheid. The 110th Antitank Company (minus a platoon at Hosingen) and nine 707th Tank Battalion tanks (six with 105mm howitzers) defended Hoscheid until the afternoon of the 17th when the tanks and as many soldiers as they could carry escaped to Wiltz.

Lead elements of the 15th Parachute slipped between the Company E and F strong points. Company G from Brandenburg managed to contain this penetration and Colonel James Rudder, commanding the 109th, also sent C Company to Brandenburg from his reserve, but it found no enemy.

Members of the 26th Division take cover behind a jeep while searching for snipers in the still resisting town of Fulda, Germany, April 2, 1945. The official caption states that these men belong to the 101st Infantry; however, the machine gun mount on the jeep and the M3 submachine gun held by the man on the left makes it much more likely that they are from the division reconnaissance troop.

Meanwhile the Germans were attacking Company E's strong point because it commanded a view of the river that would enable the Americans to direct artillery fire on the German crossing. Also, the 915th VG Regiment (352nd VG Division) had entered the gap between E Company and 3rd/109th (which the rest of the 352nd VG was attacking) and was approaching Diekirch. However, most of the German heavy weapons were still on the east bank of the Our, awaiting the completion of a bridge, and this enabled Colonel Rudder, with the rest of 1st/109th, a tank platoon and his two artillery battalions (elements of which fought as infantry) to halt the 915th and drive it back to Bastendorf. Meanwhile, the well-fortified 3rd/109th successfully withstood repeated attacks from the 916th VG Regiment.

Despite these misadventures, the 352nd VG managed to regroup, get its heavy weapons across the Our, advance about 2^1/$_2$ miles, and take Diekrich. To avoid encirclement the 3rd/109th had to abandon its strong points and withdraw to the southwest. By December 19, the 109th Infantry was mostly south and west of Ettelbruck. Though still generally intact it had been unable to stop the 5th Parachute Division from reaching Wiltz from protecting the southern flank of XLVII Panzer Corps.

On the same day the 28th Division temporarily ceased to exist as an integrated combat formation. Its 112th Infantry was fighting under the remnants of the 106th Division in the north. The 109th had been pushed well to the south and was essentially fighting independently. The 110th Infantry was destroyed. Its own officers estimated its losses at 2,750. The Fifth Panzer Army was finally approaching Bastogne but this advance had taken four days rather than the planned 24–36 hours. Despite the bad weather, fuel and vehicle shortages, inadequately trained personnel, and poor to nonexistent air and artillery support the Fifth Panzer Army had actually advanced a little faster than the Americans had in Operation *Cobra* when they broke out from Normandy and ultimately chased the German Army out of France. Nevertheless, this was not good enough. The Americans had time to reinforce Bastogne with the 101st Airborne Division, increasing the number of American defenders to more than 20,000. These included parts of the 9th and 10th Armored divisions plus a tank destroyer battalion, four non-divisional artillery battalions (all told, the Americans had about 130 artillery pieces in Bastogne) plus survivors from other units. Although the Germans surrounded Bastogne by December 23 they could only collect about 30,000 troops with which to attack it. Predictably they got nowhere, even though the Americans actually sustained heavier casualties. Four days later lead elements of the Third US Army broke through the German encirclement. The Germans tried to continue their offensive without Bastogne but by late December it was all over. By January 25 the Americans had recovered all their lost territory. It had cost them 105,102 casualties (including 19,246 dead and 25,806 captured and missing). German losses had been nearly as large, and they would be far less easy to replace.

6th and 25th Infantry divisions in the Philippines, February 1–6, 1945

In January 1945 General Douglas MacArthur had nearly fulfilled his promise, made in March 1942, to return and liberate the Philippine islands from Japanese occupation. In October 1944 he had landed his Sixth Army on Leyte, in the east-central part of the Philippine Archipelago, winning an important foothold. The Japanese navy's attempts to defeat MacArthur's landing ended in disaster and the loss of most of what remained of Japan's battle fleet. Most of the Japanese defenders of Leyte (mainly the 1st, 16th and 26th divisions) were lost and most of their supporting air units destroyed.

Having inflicted this heavy blow, MacArthur began a series of new landings, mostly on Luzon, the largest and most northerly of the Philippine islands. The main landing was at Lingayen Gulf on the Luzon west coast. From here, the Sixth Army's I and XIV Corps would march southward down Luzon's central plain to capture the port city of Manila, capital of the Philippines. The initial landings on January 9, 1945 were on beaches along the southern shore of Lingayen Gulf. The I Corps, with the 6th and 43rd Infantry divisions, went ashore on the eastern half of the beaches and the XIV Corps, with the 37th and 40th divisions, landed on the western half. Japanese opposition was weak and the beaches were easily secured. Soon afterwards the Americans began pushing towards Manila. The bulk of the Japanese were in the mountains east of the central plains.

The senior Japanese headquarters in the Philippines was the 14th Area Army, under the command of General Tomoyuki Yamashita. In 1941 Yamashita had led the 25th Army in its conquest of Malaya and Singapore and was recognized as one of the best generals in Japan. However, his role in the February 1936 attempt by extremist junior officers to overthrow the Imperial government, although not large enough to implicate him, had seriously harmed his reputation. Despite his success at Singapore he had been exiled to Manchuria, but was brought back to take over the Philippines when MacArthur's invasion threatened.

Yamashita had divided his forces on Luzon into three "groups" rather than the more usual armies. By far the largest of these was the 152,000-man Shobu Group under Yamashita himself. Its sector was the northern two-thirds of Luzon, beginning at the high ground east of the central plains. It included the 2nd Tank Division (minus two-thirds of its infantry), the 10th (minus the 39th Regiment), 19th, 23rd and 103rd Infantry divisions, the 58th Independent Mixed Brigade, a regimental-sized detachment from the 26th Division, and various smaller combat and service units, the latter often reorganized as provisional combat units.

The Kembu Group of 30,000 under Major General Rikichi Tsukada had the mission of defending the hills south of the central plains and of preventing the Americans from using Clark Airfield (north of Manila) for as long as possible. The 2nd Tank Division was to have joined this group and operated around Clark Airfield; however, the US landings prevented the movement of the bulk of the division to Clark. This left the Kembu Group with the 1st Raiding Group (a regimental-sized airborne infantry unit), two battalions of the 2nd Mobile Infantry (the 2nd Tank Division infantry regiment), two battalions of the 39th Infantry (10th Division), and the usual service and minor combat units. About half the group consisted of naval aviation engineers, ground crew, and antiaircraft units from the now planeless 26th Air Flotilla at Clark Airfield.

The Shimbu Group under Lieutenant General Shizuo Yokoyama held southeastern Luzon, including Manila itself and the mountains to the east and northeast. The 80,000 troops in this group included the 8th Division (minus a regiment on Leyte) and the 105th Division. Supporting units included a number of suicide boat battalions that would now fight as infantry. There were also some 20,000 navy personnel under the 31st Special Base Force in Manila.

The XIV Corps advance towards Manila encountered very little opposition until it approached the Clark Airfield complex. By the end of January it had advanced 59 miles, overrun the air bases and Fort Stotsenburg, and was pushing what remained of the Kembu Group into the Zambales Mountains to the west. However the two XIV Corps divisions found themselves strung out along a 124-mile front. The security of the corps' left flank and rear were problematic. I Corps had not kept pace with the XIV Corps' advance. It had encountered much stronger Japanese opposition from the Shobu Group and was turning east to confront it. However, reinforcements were arriving. The 25th Infantry Division and the separate 158th Regimental Combat Team (RCT), both from Sixth Army reserve, landed on January 11 and joined I Corps. The 158th RCT reinforced the 43rd Division as it attacked the Japanese defending the hills facing the east shore of Lingayen Gulf. The 25th Division took its place on the 43rd Division's right enabling the 6th Division to move further south to a position on the 25th Division's right. On January 27 the 1st Cavalry (without horses) and 32nd Infantry divisions and the separate 112th Cavalry Regiment (also without horses) came ashore. The 1st Cavalry Division reached Guimba by January 31, ready to attack towards Cabanatuan to protect the XIV Corps, left and cut Route 5 so that the Japanese could not use it for communication between the Shobu and Shimbu groups or to bring up supplies for the Shobu Group from Manila.

Route 5 was indeed of critical importance. General Yamashita knew that his forces could not stand against the Americans in open combat so his plan was to set up a huge redoubt in the mountains north of Baguio and Bambang. Here he would place his Shobu Group and part of the 105th Division from the Shimbu Group. The mountains would minimize the value of the Americans' armor, artillery, and aviation and would make their operations slow and costly. However, to stand an extended siege Yamashita needed the mountains of supplies then staged at Manila (where they had arrived from Japan) moved to his northern redoubt, especially since he did not intend to conduct a protracted defense of Manila. However, a shortage of trucks and fuel, US air and Filipino guerrilla attacks, and the frequent non-cooperation of the navy ensured that the transfer of these supplies was still far from complete at the end of January.

The main transshipment point for supplies from Manila and other depots in the central plains to the redoubt was the town of San Jose. It stood at the intersection of routes 5 and 8 and the terminus of the Manila Railway. By early January 1945 about 600 tons of supplies and equipment were arriving daily for shipment to the southeast corner of Yamashita's mountain redoubt. Unknown to him until it was too late, the commander of the Japanese 23rd Division, which, together with the 58th Independent Mixed Brigade was supposed to be defending the east and south shore of Lingayen Gulf against the I Corps, had weakened his left flank to the point where there was little to prevent a rapid American advance south towards San Jose. The arrival of the US 32nd Division to take over a sector between the 43rd and 25th divisions, allowed the 6th and 25th divisions to shift far enough south to threaten San Jose.

Although the town would come under attack much sooner than he expected or hoped, General Yamashita calculated that if he could retain San Jose for another week he could evacuate all his critical supplies. He could also enable those elements of the 105th Division, which was marching northward from the Shimbu Group to join him, to pass the town. He therefore directed Lieutenant General Yoshiharu Iwanaka, commanding the 2nd "Geki" Tank Division, to delay the American advance on San Jose. Iwanaka's division was minus a third of its tanks, its antiaircraft unit, reconnaissance regiment, two-thirds of its infantry, and part of its artillery. However, it did have one infantry battalion from the 10th Division and two from the 105th Division as attachments.

Iwanaka had little time to organize his defense. He deployed his troops among eight separate strong points located in the towns and villages. These were in ruins but still offered some cover and concealment. He did not occupy San Jose itself. Not only was it a favorite bombing target but also the Americans would have to be prevented from getting very close to it if the evacuation of supplies was to continue. Outside of the towns and villages the ground was generally flat, open, cultivated, and crisscrossed by drainage and irrigation ditches. Any attempt to maneuver in such terrain would have exposed the Japanese to American air strikes and artillery fire. Therefore, the Japanese dug in their tanks (which in any case were no match for their American counterparts) and tried to cover the open areas by fire.

The I Corps plan to capture San Jose was simplicity itself. The 25th Division, reinforced with a 155mm gun battalion, an 8in. howitzer battalion, a 4.2in. mortar company, and a medium tank company, would attack down Route 8

US infantrymen return enemy fire on Japanese positions in the Intramurce section of Manila, Philippines, February 23, 1945. Each of the three soldiers on the right is firing a BAR.

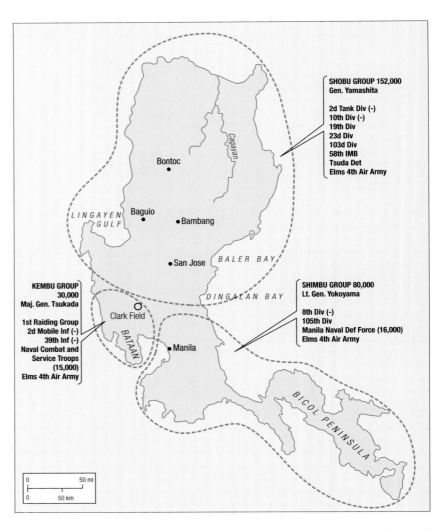

SHOBU GROUP 152,000
Gen. Yamashita

2d Tank Div (-)
10th Div (-)
19th Div
23d Div
103d Div
58th IMB
Tsuda Det
Elms 4th Air Army

KEMBU GROUP
30,000
Maj. Gen. Tsukada

1st Raiding Group
2d Mobile Inf (-)
39th Inf (-)
Naval Combat and
Service Troops
(15,000)
Elms 4th Air Army

SHIMBU GROUP 80,000
Lt. Gen. Yokoyama

8th Div (-)
105th Div
Manila Naval Def Force (16,000)
Elms 4th Air Army

through the Japanese defenders in Umingan, Lupao, and San Isidro, and approach San Jose from the northwest. The 6th Division, reinforced with two 105mm and one 155mm howitzer battalions, a 4.2in. mortar company, a medium tank company, and two light tank platoons, would attack up Route 5 through Muñoz to approach the town from the southwest.

On the morning of February 1 the Americans began their offensive as the 20th Infantry (Regiment) from the 6th Division attacked Muñoz while the 27th Infantry (25th Division) assaulted Umingan. The Japanese defended Muñoz with a task force of about 2,000 formed around the 6th Tank Regiment (with only three of its five tank companies present), some artillery and antitank guns, and about half of the 356th Independent Infantry Battalion (105th Division). Holding Umingan was the 3rd Battalion of the 26th Independent Mixed Regiment (IMR) reinforced with a rifle company from the 10th Division, some tanks (apparently, from the 26th IMR Tank Unit), and some antitank guns and 75mm field guns. The 26th IMR was attached to the 105th Division.

Both American attacks were soon stopped cold. The troops could not advance across the open ground and the tanks supporting the 27th Infantry's attack could not maneuver off the roads because of the irrigation ditches. The next day at Muñoz the 20th Infantry made only slight gains. In the north the commander of the 25th Division, Major General Charles Mullins, ordered the 35th Infantry to bypass Umingan to the south. Using single-lane dirt roads one

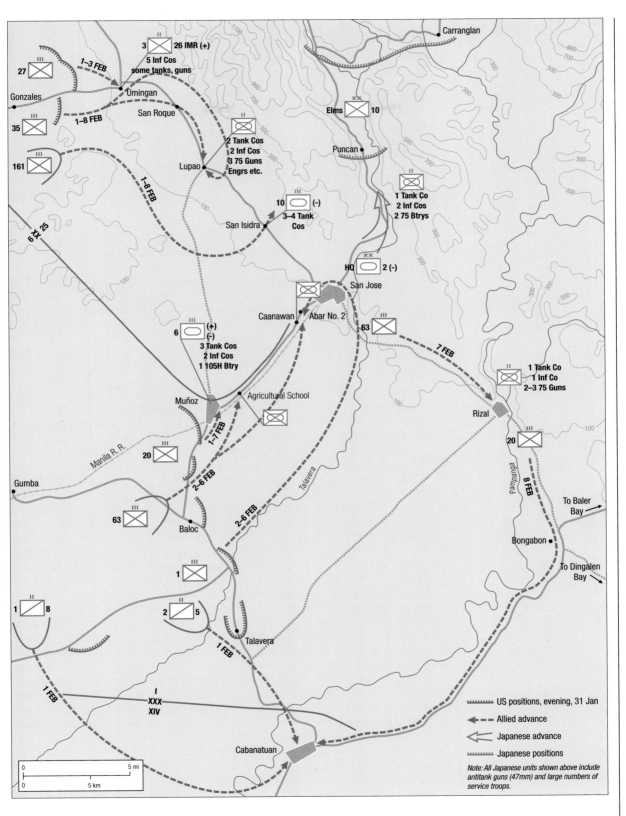

The capture of San Jose, Luzon, the Philippines, February 1–8, 1945.

M1918 155mm howitzers of C Battery, 218th Field Artillery Battalion fire in support of infantry advancing on Japanese positions in Arare, New Guinea, May 25, 1944. Although the M1 howitzer had officially superseded the M1918 many of these older howitzers continued to serve (especially in the Pacific Theater) until the end of the war. The M1918 weighed 8,184 lb. and had a range of upto 12,400 yards. For further details see Battle Orders 17, *US Army Infantry Divisions 1942–43*.

battalion reached the San Roque barrio on Route 8, four miles southeast of Umingan. The other two attacked Umingan through its southeast corner that evening. Next day, they did not meet the resistance they expected. The previous night most of the Japanese had withdrawn northeast towards the Caraballo Mountains. They had left behind a rear guard (who were not completely eliminated until February 3), eight antitank guns, and large supplies of 75mm and 47mm ammunition. The Americans had lost 43 killed and 143 wounded. About 150 Japanese reportedly died. The town had taken a day longer to capture than expected.

General Mullins then ordered the 27th Infantry to mop up the Japanese still in Umingan while the 35th Infantry attacked Lupao. The 35th Infantry estimated that only a rifle company and a few tanks defended Lupao so on February 2 it sent only one battalion to attack it. In fact the defenders were a battalion-sized task force drawn from three different regiments. When the Americans got to within 750 yards of the town they came under intense Japanese fire and were immediately halted. The open terrain frustrated their attempts to outflank the town. Frontal attacks by the full regiment next day (February 3) failed to achieve results.

In the south, 6th Division commander Major General Edwin Patrick had relieved the 20th Infantry commander for his lack of progress, but this brought no improvement. Therefore in the late afternoon of February 1 he ordered the 1st Infantry to reconnoiter the Talavera River and find an overland approach to the point at which the San Jose–Rizal road crosses the river about three miles southeast of San Jose. The 1st Infantry could then attack San Jose from there. Patrick also ordered the 63rd Infantry to bypass Muñoz to the southeast (but to the left of the 1st Infantry), and come back on Route 5 north of the town ready to advance on San Jose from there. This move would be made in concert with the 1st Infantry.

Meanwhile, General Mullins decided to bypass Lupao. Leaving the 27th Infantry in Umingan and the 35th Infantry to clear Lupao he ordered the 161st Infantry to move cross-country to Route 8 midway between Lupao and San Jose. Once there it was to be ready, if needed, to assist the 6th Division in capturing San Jose. It would also block Japanese movement between San Jose and Lupao. The 161st reached Route 8 by mid-afternoon of February 4. It set up its roadblock and was ready to attack either northwest towards San Isidro or southeast towards San Jose. However, the progress made by the 6th Division and the 35th Infantry soon made its efforts unnecessary.

At about the same time the 3rd/35th Infantry enveloped Lupao from the east by moving to a point on Route 8 about 1,500 yards to the southeast side of the town. The battalion reached this position during the afternoon of February 3 and next day forced its way into the southeast edge of Lupao against strong opposition. Unfortunately, the 35th Infantry elements north and west of the town were still unable to make any progress.

In the afternoon of February 2, following a sharp skirmish with a Japanese tank-infantry patrol, lead elements of the 1st Infantry reached the crossing of the Talavera River southeast of San Jose. By late afternoon next day the 1st Infantry occupied two positions south and east of San Jose. Meanwhile on February 2 the 63rd Infantry reached Route 5 near an agricultural school held by a small Japanese tank-infantry group. Leaving a reinforced company to deal with these Japanese the regiment advanced up Route 5 next afternoon and by dusk was in sight of the Barrios Caanawan and Abar No. 2, both held by small Japanese detachments. That evening General Patrick ordered both the 1st and 63rd Infantry to attack San Jose on the 4th.

Both regiments were expecting a stiff fight, but although Japanese resistance near Abar No. 2 held up the 63rd infantry, two companies of the 1st Infantry entered San Jose against almost no opposition. Its losses were only two killed and 25 wounded, including one killed and seven wounded by a "friendly" air strike.

Since San Jose could no longer be defended, on February 4 General Yamashita ordered a general withdrawal of Japanese forces from the area. However this order did not reach Muñoz (still besieged by the 20th Infantry) or Rizal until February 6 after the troops in Lupao and Muñoz were already trapped. About 50 Fifth Air Force aircraft and all of the 6th Division's organic and attached artillery pounded Muñoz. The Muñoz garrison tried to escape up Route 5 next day but was destroyed. Its losses (including those of the detachments at the barrios and agricultural school) totaled 52 tanks, 16 antitank guns, four 105mm howitzers, and 1,500 (out of 2,000) men. The troops in Lupao tried to break out the next night. Five tanks escaped, though they had to be abandoned later. A few hundred troops got out as well but 900, plus 33 tanks and three 75mm guns, were lost. The Japanese abandoned San Isidro on the night of February 5/6 before the 161st Infantry could attack it, leaving behind 23 tanks and most of their guns. The 161st killed more than 100 Japanese stragglers.

Though they failed to hold San Jose for as long as they had hoped, the Japanese had achieved their key objectives. The sacrificial defense of Muñoz and Lupao had bought enough time to evacuate the essential supplies from San Jose and to enable a sufficient portion of the 105th Division to join the Shobu Group. On the debit side, their piecemeal and passive defense dispelled all American anxieties about a counterattack from the east and left XVI Corps free to march on Manila. Also, Japanese losses had been very heavy. The 2nd Tank Division had lost 180 of the 220 tanks available on January 9 and 2,250 of the 6,500 men that defended San Jose. It would never fight again as a tank division. The threat posed by Japanese tanks, such as it was, had ceased to exist.

A 60mm mortar squad from Company C, 1st Battalion, 158th Infantry (a separate infantry regiment not attached to any division) in action on Noemfoor Island, July 2, 1944. The M2 60mm mortar weighed 42 lb. and could fire its 3 lb. shells out to nearly 2,000 yards. For further details see Battle Orders 17, *US Army Infantry Divisions 1942–43*.

Lessons learned

In June 1945, the AGF rolled out a new set of organization tables for a 15,838-man infantry division intended for the planned invasion of Japan. The Army had long chafed under the strict economy regime imposed by General McNair and his "no-men" even though it had enabled the Army to field just enough divisions to get it through the war. The surrender of Nazi Germany allowed many divisions to be deactivated. The manpower thus released enabled the AGF to address the combat theaters' bitterest complaints about the shortfalls of its divisions. It made the division military police platoon a company and enlarged the division signal company by nearly 30 percent. It converted the division artillery to six guns per howitzer battery rather than four. Since the same command and logistical structure could serve the larger batteries, this meant a 50 percent firepower increase at a very modest cost in additional vehicles and manpower.

It was the infantry regiment, however, that underwent the biggest change. Its antitank and cannon companies became miniature tank companies with nine tanks each. Those in the antitank company would have 90mm guns while those in the cannon company would have 105mm howitzers. The AGF considered standard 17-tank companies but, given that the division would probably also have an attached tank battalion, this configuration would have given an infantry division nearly as many medium tanks as an armored division. The antitank mine platoon would move to the regimental headquarters company. The regimental service company was augmented so it could support the tanks. The regimental headquarters company acquired a counterfire section to pinpoint trench mortars of the kind that the Germans had used against the Americans so effectively. Infantry battalion headquarters companies gave up their antitank platoons to the weapons companies. The antitank platoons themselves became gun platoons when they replaced their 57mm guns with six of the new M20 75mm recoilless rifles. Rifle company weapons platoons more than doubled in size. Each of them picked up an officer assistant platoon leader, a section of three M18 57mm recoilless rifles (structured like the 60mm mortar section), and an assault section of three six-man squads, with two bazookas each. The wartime performance of ad hoc bazooka teams had convinced the AGF that bazooka teams should be permanent. The recoilless rifles had only been used in the Pacific Theater but they had done well against Japanese fortifications on Okinawa. Testing revealed a disappointing antitank performance though even in this they were better than the 57mm guns they replaced.

In October 1945 General Eisenhower set up a General Board to study the lessons of the war from a European Theater standpoint. The board proposed an infantry division of 20,578 that, among other things, included its own tank regiment but no more actual infantry than the 14,037-man wartime division had. Had such divisions been in use in 1944 they would probably have delayed D-Day by at least a year. In 1948 with the publication of tables for a postwar division of 18,804 with 135 medium or heavy tanks the Army had finally rejected General McNair's system of economies.

An M8 reconnaissance armored car of the 30th Infantry Division rolls through the streets of Kinsweiler, Germany, November 21, 1944. In the left background a disabled German Sturmgeschütz III Ausf. G has been pushed into a ditch to clear the road. The M8 weighed 17,400 lb. and carried a 37mm antitank gun and a coaxial machine gun in an open-topped turret.

Bibliography

Published books

Thomas Berndt, *Standard Catalog of US Military Vehicles 1940–65*, Krause Publications, Iola, WI 1995.

Hugh M. Cole, *United States Army in World War II – The European Theater of Operations – The Ardennes: Battle of the Bulge*, Historical Division US Army, Washington, DC, 1988.

David Doyle, *Standard Catalog of US Military Vehicles 2nd Edition*, Krause Publications, Iola, WI 2003.

Trevor N. Dupuy, *Hitler's Last Gamble, the Battle of the Bulge, December 1944 – January 1945*, Harper-Collins Publishers, 1994.

Chris Ellis and Peter Chamberlain, *American Armored Cars 1940–1945*, Almarks Publications, Edgware, Middlesex, UK, 1969.

Kent Roberts Greenfield, Robert R. Palmer, and Bell I. Wiley, *United States Army in World War II – The Army Ground Forces – The Organization of Ground Combat Troops*, Historical Division US Army, Washington, DC, 1947.

Gordon A. Harrison, *United States Army in World War II – The European Theater of Operations – Cross-Channel Attack*, Historical Division US Army, Washington, DC, 1989.

Ian V. Hogg, *British and American Artillery of World War II*, Hippocrene Books, NY, 1978.

George F. Nafziger, *The German Order of Battle, Panzers and Artillery in World War II*, Stackpole Books, Harrisburg, PA, and Greenhill Books, London, UK, 1995.

George F. Nafziger, *The German Order of Battle, Infantry in World War II*, Stackpole Books, Harrisburg, PA, and Greenhill Books, London, UK, 2000.

Robert Ross Smith, *United States Army in World War II – The War in the Pacific – Triumph in the Philippines*, Historical Division US Army, Washington, DC, 1984.

General Staff, Southwest Pacific Area, *Reports of General MacArthur, The Campaigns of MacArthur in the Pacific*, Volume I and *Japanese Operations in the Southwest Pacific Area*, Volume II Part 2, US Government Printing Office, Washington, DC, 1966.

Shelby L. Stanton, *Order of Battle, the US Army in World War II*, Presidio Press, Novato, CA, 1984.

Niklas Zetterling, *Normandy 1944, German Military Organization*, Combat Power and Organizational Effectiveness, J.J. Fedorowicz Publishing, 2000.

Articles in periodicals

LTC Bruce Palmer, Jr., "New Battle Lessons on Reconnaissance," *Cavalry Journal* Vol. LII No. 5, Washington, DC, October 1943.

Cavalry School Staff, "Reconnaissance," *Cavalry Journal* Vol. LII No. 5, Washington, DC, October 1943.

Office of the Chief of Infantry, "The Service Company", *Infantry Journal* Vol. L No. 6, Washington, DC, June 1941.

MAJ John F. Bird, FA, "The Forward Observer," *The Field Artillery Journal* Vol. 31 No. 7, Washington, DC, July 1941.

CPT J. J. Davis, FA, "Fire Direction Decentralized," *The Field Artillery Journal* Vol. 32 No. 3, Washington, DC, March 1942.

LTC H. D. Kehm, FA, "Artillery Ammunition Supply," *The Field Artillery Journal* Vol. 32 No. 4, Washington, DC, April 1942.

LT Angus Rutledge, FA, "What About the Service Battery?" *The Field Artillery Journal* Vol. 32 No. 4, Washington, DC, April 1942.

Infantry School Staff, "Supply – An Infantry School Teaching," *The Infantry School Mailing List* Vol. XXII, Fort Benning, GA, October 1941.

Infantry School Staff, "Organization and Use of the Infantry Communication System," *The Infantry School Mailing List* Vol. XXVII, Fort Benning, GA, February 1944.

Infantry School Staff, "Combat Training: The Cannon Platoon in the Attack," *The Infantry School Mailing List* Vol. XXVII, Fort Benning, GA, February 1944.

Infantry School Staff, "Infantry Radio Communication," *The Infantry School Mailing List* Vol. XXIX, Fort Benning, GA, October 1946.

Infantry School Staff, "Infantry Weapons," *The Infantry School Mailing List* Vol. XXX, Fort Benning, GA, April 1947.

Infantry School Staff, "Engineer Combat Battalion (Infantry Division)," *The Infantry School Mailing List* Vol. XXIX, Fort Benning, GA, October 1946.

Websites

www.gordon.army.mil/ocos/museum Official US Army Signal Corps website.

www.greenradio.de/e_bc611.htm Describes the SCR-536.

www.greenradio.de/e_bc728.htm Describes the SCR-543/593.

www.kpjung.de/e_kplc.htm Describes WWII-era, vehicle-mounted radios.

www.kpjung.de/e_pogo.htm Describes the SCR-511 man-pack radio.

www.kpjung.de/e_bc1000.htm Describes the SCR-300 man-pack radio.

www.vectorsite.net/ttwizb.html An essay on WWII radio communication technology.

www.associated-ind.com/pdf/field_wire.pdf A PDF download covering field telephones and associated equipment.

www.labradorman.com/Reenacting/Research/WW2_Communications.htm Excellent site covering a wide range of US WWII radios.

www.korean-war/Russia/KoreaPoligonApp-54.html A site devoted to a Russian history of the Korean War, but including many factual details on late World War II US radios.

www.jproc.ca/crypto/m94.html Describes the M-94 encryption device.

www.en-wikipedia.org/wiki/M-209 Describes the M209 mechanical cipher machine.

www.maritime.org/csp1500inst.htm Technical manual for the M-209.

www.radiomilitari.com/scr506.html Describes the SCR-506 vehicular radio.

www.nj7p.org/cgi-bin/millist2?mode=toc The new military list database; contains information on a wide variety of military radios.

Appendix

Appendix 1: Tables of organization

All tables published by the War Department, Washington, DC on March 1, 1943, July 15, 1943 and on the dates noted below (with changes).

TO 2-67	Cavalry Reconnaissance Troop, Mechanized, Infantry Division
TO 5-15	Engineer Combat Battalion, Infantry Division (March 13, 1944)
TO 5-16	Headquarters & Headquarters and Service Company, Engineer Combat Battalion, Infantry Division (March 13, 1944)
TO 5-17	Engineer Combat Company or Engineer Combat Troop (March 13, 1944)
TO 6-10	Division Artillery, Motorized, Infantry Division (February 26 and September 27, 1944)
TO 6-10-1	Headquarters & Headquarters Battery, Division Artillery, Motorized, Infantry Division (September 27, 1944)
TO 6-25	Field Artillery Battalion, Light, Truck-Drawn (September 27, 1944)
TO 6-325	Field Artillery Battalion, Light, Tractor-Drawn (July 26, 1943 and October 20, 1944)
TO 6-26	Headquarters & Headquarters Battery, Field Artillery
TO 6-325	Field Artillery Battery, 105mm Howitzer, Tractor-Drawn (July 26, 1943 and October 20, 1944)
TO 6-329	Service Battery, Field Artillery Battalion, Light, Tractor-Drawn (July 26, 1943 and October 20, 1944)
TO 6-335	Field Artillery Battery, Motorized, 155mm Howitzer or 4.5in. Gun, Tractor-Drawn (July 3, 1943 and September 27, 1944)
TO 6-339	Service Battery, Motorized, Field Artillery Battalion, Motorized, 155mm Howitzer or 4.5in. Gun, Truck-Drawn (July 3, 1943 and September 27, 1944)
TO 7	Infantry Division (January 13, 1945)
TO 7-1	Headquarters, Infantry Division (January 13, 1945)
TO 7-2	Headquarters Company, Infantry Division (January 13, 1945)
TO 7-11	Infantry Regiment (February 26, 1944)
TO 7-12	Headquarters & Headquarters Company, Infantry Regiment (February 26, 1944)
TO 7-13	Service Company, Infantry Regiment (February 26, 1944)
TO 7-14	Infantry Cannon Company (February 26, 1944)
TO 7-14S	Infantry Cannon Company, Self-Propelled (February 26, 1944)
TO 7-15	Infantry Battalion (February 12, 1944)
TO 7-16	Headquarters & Headquarters Company, Infantry Battalion (February 26, 1944)
TO 7-17	Infantry Rifle Company (February 26, 1944)
TO 7-18	Infantry Heavy Weapons Company (February 26, 1944)
TO 7-117	Infantry Antitank Company (February 26, 1944)
TO 8-15	Medical Battalion (February 14, 1945)
TO 8-16	Headquarters & Headquarters Detachment, Medical Battalion (February 14, 1945)
TO 8-17	Collecting Company, Medical Battalion (February 14, 1945)
TO 8-18	Clearing Company, Medical Battalion (February 14, 1945)
TO 9-8	Ordnance Light Maintenance Company, Infantry Division (November 17, 1944)
TO 10-17	Quartermaster Company, Infantry Division (February 19, 1944)
TO 11-7	Signal Company, Infantry Division (December 11, 1943)
TO 19-7	Military Police Platoon, Infantry Division (March 26 and September 12, 1944)

Appendix 2: US infantry divisions, compositio and combat records

Division	Infantry [1]	Artillery [2]	Divisional units [3]	Activated	Overseas [4]
1st	16th Infantry 18th Infantry 26th Infantry	5th Bn (155) 7th Bn (105) 32d Bn (105) 33d Bn (105)	1st Engineer Bn 1st Medical Bn 1st Recon Troop 1st QM Bn (Co) 1st Signal Co	8 Aug 17	1–7 Aug 42 (to UK)
2d	9th Infantry 23d Infantry 38th Infantry	12th Bn (155) 15th Bn (105) 37th Bn (105) 38th Bn (105)	2d Engineer Bn 2d Medical Bn 2d Recon Troop 2d QM Bn (Co) 2d Signal Co	26 Oct 17	8–18 Sep 43 (to UK) 20 Jul 45 (arrived NY
3d	7th Infantry 15th Infantry 30th Infantry	9th Bn (155) 10th Bn (105) 39th Bn (105) 41st Bn (105)	10th Engineer Bn 3d Medical Bn 3d Recon Troop 3d QM Bn (Co) 3d Signal Co	28 Nov 17	27 Oct to 8 Nov 42 (to Fedala, N Africa)
4th (motorized division from 27 Aug 41 to 4 Aug 43)	8th Infantry 12th Infantry from 24 Oct 41 22d Infantry	20th Bn (155) 29th Bn (105) 42d Bn (105) 44th Bn (105)	4th Engineer Bn 4th Medical Bn 4th Recon Troop 4th QM Bn (Co) 4th Signal Co	1 Jul 40. Activated at Fort Benning, GA	18–26 Jan 44 (to UK) 10 Jul 45 (arrived NYC)
5th	2d Infantry 10th Infantry 11th Infantry	19th Bn (105) 21st Bn (155) 46th Bn (105) 50th Bn (105)	7th Engineer Bn 5th Medical Bn 5th Recon Troop 5th QM Bn (Co) 5th Signal Co	16 Oct 39. Activated at Fort McClellan, AL	30 Apr to 11 May 42 (Iceland); 7 Aug 43 (UK) 19 Jul 45 (arr. Boston MA)
6th (motorized division from 9 Apr 42 to 21 May 43)	1st Infantry 20th Infantry 63d Infantry from 1 Jun 41	1st Bn (105) 51st Bn (105) 53d Bn (105) 80th Bn (155)	6th Engineer Bn 6th Medical Bn 6th Recon Troop 6th QM Bn (Co) 6th Signal Co	10 Oct 39. Activated at Fort Lewis, WA	21–29 Jul 43 (to Hawaii)
7th (motorized division from 9 Apr 42 to 1 Jan 43)	17th Infantry 32d Infantry 53d Inf to 7 Nov 41 159th (CANG) 29 Sep 41 to 23 Aug 43 184th (CANG) from 23 Aug 43	31st Bn (155) 48th Bn (105) 49th Bn (105) 57th Bn (105)	13th Engineer Bn 7th Medical Bn 7th Recon Troop 7th QM Bn (Co) 7th Signal Co	1 Jul 40. Activated at Fort Ord, CA	24 Apr to 11 May 43 (to Aleutians)
8th (motorized division from 9 Apr 42 to 15 May 43)	13th Infantry 28th Infantry 34th Inf to 12 Jun 43 121st (GANG) from 22 Nov 41	28th Bn (155) 43d Bn (105) 45th Bn (105) 56th Bn (105)	12th Engineer Bn 8th Medical Bn 8th Recon Troop 8th QM Bn (Co) 8th Signal Co	1 Jul 40. Activated at Camp Jackson, SC	5–15 Dec 43 (to UK); 10 Jul 45 (arrived Hampton Roads)

Combat [5]	Campaigns [6]	Casualties [7]	Aug 45 location [8]
8 Nov 42 landed in N Africa	NA-1, NA-2, IT-1, EU-1, EU-2, EU-4, EU-5, EU-6	TBC: 20,659 KIA: 3,616 WIA: 15,208 (664) POW: 1,336 (19) MIA: 499 (66)	Ansbach, Germany
7 Jun 44 landed in France; first combat 8 Jun 44	EU-1, EU-2, EU-4, EU-5, EU-6	TBC: 16,795 KIA: 3,031 WIA: 12,785 (457) POW: 786 (9) MIA: 193 (15)	Camp Swift, TX
8 Nov 42 landed in N Africa	NA-1, NA-2, IT-1, IT-2, IT-3, IT-4, EU-3, EU-4, EU-5, EU-6	TBC: 25,977 KIA: 4,922 WIA: 18,766 (636) POW: 1,735 (11) MIA: 554 (65)	Salzburg, Austria
6 Jun 44 assaulted Utah Beach with 359th Infantry, 90th Division, attached	EU-1, EU-2, EU-4, EU-5, EU-6	TBC: 22,660 KIA: 4,097 WIA: 17,371 (757) POW: 731 (11) MIA: 461 (42)	Camp Butner, NC
11 Jul 44 landed at Utah Beach, Normandy; first combat 13 Jul 44	EU-1, EU-2, EU-4, EU-5, EU-6	TBC: 12,818 KIA: 2,298 WIA: 9,549 (358) POW: 683 (3) MIA: 288 (25)	Camp Campbell, KY
31 Jan 44 Milne Bay New Guinea; first combat 30 Jul 44, Sansapor New Guinea	PA-5, PA-9	TBC: 2,370 KIA: 410 WIA: 1,957 (104) POW: 0 MIA: 3 (3)	Bagabag, Philippines
11 May 43 assaulted Attu, Aleutian Islands	PA-2, PA-8 (Kwajalein), PA-9, PA-11	TBC: 9,212 KIA: 1,948 WIA: 7,258 (386) POW: 2 (2) MIA: 4 (1)	Okinawa
3 Jul 44 landed at Utah Beach, Normandy; first combat 12 Jul 44	EU-1, EU-2, EU-4, EU-6	TBC: 13,986 KIA: 2,532 WIA: 10,057 (288) POW: 668 (5) MIA: 729 (27)	Ft Leonard Wood, MO

9th	39th Infantry 47th Infantry 60th Infantry	26th Bn (105) 34th Bn (155) 60th Bn (105) 84th Bn (105)	15th Engineer Bn 9th Medical Bn 9th Recon Troop 9th QM Bn (Co) 9th Signal Co	1 Aug 40. Activated at Fort Bragg, NC	11–25 Dec 42 (N Africa)
24th	19th Infantry 21st Infantry 299th (HING) to 21 Jul 42 298th (HING) 23 Jul 42 to 12 Jun 43 34th Inf from 12 Jun 43	11th Bn (155) 13th Bn (105) 52d Bn (105) 63d Bn (105)	3d Engineer Bn 24th Medical Bn 24th Recon Troop 24th QM Bn (Co) 24th Signal Co	1 Oct 41. Redesignated from the Hawaiian Division at Schofield Barracks, HI	7 Dec 41 (on Hawaii)
25th	27th Infantry 35th Infantry 298th (HING) to 23 Jul 42 161st (WANG) from 23 Jul 42	8th Bn (105) 64th Bn (105) 89th Bn (105) 90th Bn (155)	65th Engineer Bn 25th Medical Bn 25th Recon Troop 25th QM Bn (Co) 25th Signal Co	1 Oct 41. Formed from a brigade of the Hawaiian Division at Barracks, HI	7 Dec 41 (on Hawaii)
26th MANG	101st (MANG) 104th (MANG) 182d (MANG) to 14 Jan 42 181st (MANG) to 27 Jan 43 328th Inf from 12 Feb 43	101st Bn* (105) 102d Bn* (105) 180th Bn* (155) 263d Bn (105)	101st Engineer Bn 114th Medical Bn 26th Recon Troop 26th QM Bn (Co) 26th Signal Co	16 Jan 41. Inducted into Federal service at Boston, MA	27 Aug to 7 Sep 44 (landed at Cherbourg & Utah Beach, Normandy)
27th NYNG	105th (NYNG) 106th (NYNG) 108th (NYNG) to 1 Sep 42 165th (NYNG) in 40th Inf Div 1 Sep 42 to 30 Oct 42 only 160th (CANG) 1 Sep 42 to 30 Oct 42	104th Bn* (105) 105th Bn* (105) 106th Bn* (155) 249th Bn (105)	102d Engineer Bn 102d Medical Bn 27th Recon Troop 27th QM Bn (Co) 27th Signal Co	15 Oct 40. Inducted into Federal service at New York, NY	10–20 Mar 42 (to Hawaii)
28th PANG	109th (PANG) 110th (PANG) 111th (PANG to 17 Feb 42 112th (PANG)	107th Bn* (105) 108th Bn* (155) 109th Bn* (105) 229th Bn (105)	103d Engineer Bn 103d Medical Bn 28th Recon Troop 28th QM Bn (Co) 28th Signal Co	17 Feb 41. Inducted into Federal service at Philadelphia, PA	8–18 Oct 43 (to UK)
29th VA, MD, PA, & DC NG	115th (MDNG) 116th (VANG) 175th (MDNG) 176th (VANG) to 11 Mar 42	110th Bn* (105) 111th Bn* (105) 224th Bn (105) 227th Bn (155)	121st Engineer Bn 104th Medical Bn 29th Recon Troop 29th QM Bn (Co) 29th Signal Co	3 Feb 41. Inducted into Federal service at Washington, DC	5–11 Oct 42 (to UK)

8 Nov 42 the inf. regiments landed in N Africa but div HQ did not land until 25 Dec 42	NA-1, NA-2, IT-1, EU-1, EU-2, EU-4, EU-5, EU-6	TBC: 23,277 KIA: 3,856 WIA: 17,416 (648) POW: 1,648 (13) MIA: 357 (33)	Bayreuth, Germany
7 Dec 41, present at Pearl Harbor attack	PA-1, PA-5, PA-9	TBC: 7,012 KIA: 1,374 WIA: 5,621 (315) POW: 6 (1) MIA: 11 (1)	Davao, Mindanao, Philippines
7 Dec 41, present at Pearl Harbor attack	PA-1, PA-4, PA-6, PA-9	TBC: 5,432 KIA: 1,235 WIA: 4,190 (262) POW: 2 (0) MIA: 5 (3)	Bambam, Philippines
7 Sep 44 landed in Normandy; first combat 7 Oct 44	EU-2, EU-4, EU-5, EU-6	TBC: 10,701 KIA: 1,850 WIA: 7,886 (262) POW: 806 (17) MIA: 159 (7)	Passau, Germany
165th & 3/105 assaulted Makin 20 Nov 43; full division first fought at Saipan from 16 Jun 44	PA-1, PA-10, PA-11	TBC: 6,533 KIA: 1,512 WIA: 4,980 (332) POW: 1 (0) MIA: 40 (5)	Okinawa
22 Jul 44 landed in Normandy and was in action the next day	EU-1, EU-2, EU-4, EU-5, EU-6	TBC: 16,762 KIA: 2,316 WIA: 9,609 (367) POW: 3,953 (87) MIA: 884 (103)	Kaiserslautern, Germany
6 Jun 44 landed at Omaha Beach, Normandy	EU-1, EU-2, EU-4, EU-6	TBC: 20,620 KIA: 3,887 WIA: 15,541 (899) POW: 845 (6) MIA: 347 (32)	Warendorf, Germany

30th NC, SC, GA, & TN NG	117th (TNNG) 118th (SCNG) to 24 Aug 42 120th (NCNG) 121st (GANG) to 22 Nov 41 119th (NCNG) from 1 Sep 42	113th Bn* (155) 118th Bn* (105) 197th Bn (105) 230th Bn (105)	105th Engineer Bn 105th Medical Bn 30th Recon Troop 30th QM Bn (Co) 30th Signal Co	16 Sep 40. Inducted into Federal service at Ft Jackson, SC	11–23 Feb 44 (to UK
31st LA, MS, AL, & FL NG	124th (FLNG) to 15 Dec 41 155th (MSNG) 156th (LANG) 167th (ALNG) 154th Infantry 15 Dec 41 to 5 Apr 44 then reformed as 124th Infantry	114th Bn* (155) 116th Bn* (105) 117th Bn* (105) 149th Bn (105)	106th Engineer Bn 106th Medical Bn 31st Recon Troop 31st QM Bn (Co) 31st Signal Co	25 Nov 40. Inducted into Federal service at Birmingham, AL	13 Mar to 24 Apr 44 (to Dobodura, New Guinea for jungle training)
32d MI & WI NG	125th (MING) to 8 Dec 41 126th (MING) 127th (MING) 128th (WING)	120th Bn* (105) 121st Bn* (155) 126th Bn* (105) 129th Bn (105)	114th Engineer Bn 107th Medical Bn 32d Recon Troop 32d QM Bn (Co) 32d Signal Co	15 Oct 40. Inducted into Federal service at Lansing, MI	22 Apr to 14 May 42 (to Australia)
33d ILNG	129th (ILNG) to 31 Jul 43 130th (ILNG) 131st (ILNG) to 21 Feb 42 132d (ILNG) to 14 Jan 42 123d Inf from 28 Sep 42 136th Inf from 1 Apr 42	122d Bn* (105) 123d Bn* (155) 124th Bn* (105) 210th Bn (105)	108th Engineer Bn 108th Medical Bn 33d Recon Troop 33d QM Bn (Co) 33d Signal Co	5 Mar 41. Inducted into Federal service at Chicago, IL	7–12 Jul 43 (to Hawaii)
34th ND, SD, IA, & MN NG	133d (IANG) 135th (MNNG) 164th (NDNG) to 8 Dec 41 168th (IANG)	125th Bn* (105) 151st Bn* (105) 175th Bn (105) 185th Bn* (155)	109th Engineer Bn 109th Medical Bn 34th Recon Troop 34th QM Bn (Co) 34th Signal Co	10 Feb 41. Inducted into Federal service at Council Bluffs, IA	14–31 Jan 42 (to Northern Ireland) landed in N Africa 3 Jan 43
35th KS, MO, & NE NG	134th (NENG) 137th (KSNG) 138th (MONG) to 3 Feb 42 140th (MONG) to 27 Jan 43 320th Inf from 26 Jan 43	127th Bn* (155) 161st Bn* (105) 216th Bn (105) 219th Bn (105)	60th Engineer Bn 110th Medical Bn 35th Recon Troop 35th QM Bn (Co) 35th Signal Co	23 Dec 40. Inducted into Federal service at Lincoln, NE	12–26 May 44 (to UK)
36th TXNG	141st (TXNG) 142d (TXNG) 143d (TXNG) 144th (TXNG) to 1 Feb 42	131st Bn* (105) 132d Bn* (105) 133d Bn* (105) 155th Bn (155)	111th Engineer Bn 111th Medical Bn 36th Recon Troop 36th QM Bn (Co) 36th Signal Co	25 Nov 40. Inducted into Federal service at San Antonio, TX	2–13 Apr 43 (to N Africa)

10 Jun 44 landed in Normandy; in action the next day	EU-1, EU-2, EU-4, EU-5, EU-6	TBC: 18,446 KIA: 3,003 WIA: 13,376 (513) POW: 1,164 (8) MIA: 357 (33)	Wolmarstadt, Germany
5–14 Jul 44 division landed in Aitape (124th Inf), Toem (167th Inf), & Sarmi-Wadke areas of New Guinea	PA-5, PA-9	TBC: 1,733 KIA: 340 WIA: 1,392 (74) POW: 1 (1) MIA: 0	Valencia, Mindanao, Philippines
128th Inf landed in Papua New Guinea 15–28 Sep 42; the rest of the division was in action by 19 Nov 42	PA-3, PA-5, PA-9	TBC: 7,268 KIA: 1,613 WIA: 5,627 (372) POW: 1 (0) MIA: 27 (17)	Anabat, Philippines
11 May 44 landed at Finschhafen, NG but mostly for garrison duty and training; first real combat was on Luzon from 19 Feb 45	PA-5, PA-9	TBC: 2,426 KIA: 396 WIA: 2,024 (128) POW: 1 (0) MIA: 5 (0)	Baguio, Philippines
168th Inf assaulted Algiers 8 Nov 42; full division in action in Tunisia by 11 Feb 43	NA-1 (168th Infantry only), NA-2, IT-2, IT-3, IT-5, IT-6	TBC: 16,401 KIA: 2,866 WIA: 11,545 (484) POW: 1,368 (20) MIA: 622 (38)	Iseo, Italy
6 Jul 44 landed over Omaha Beach, Normandy; was in action by 11 Jul 44	EU-1, EU-2, EU-4, EU-5, EU-6	TBC: 15,822 KIA: 2,485 WIA: 11,526 (462) POW: 1,471 (26) MIA: 340 (24)	Hamborn, Germany
9 Sep 43 assaulted Salerno	IT-2, IT-3, IT-4, EU-3, EU-4, EU-5, EU-6	TBC: 19,466 KIA: 3,131 WIA: 13,191 (506) POW: 2,650 (18) MIA: 622 (38)	Kufstein, Austria

37th OHNG	145th (OHNG) 147th (OHNG) to 4/6/42 (7/31/43)[9] 148th (OHNG) to 1/16/42 166th (OHNG) 129th (ILNG) attached 9/19/42 then organic from 7/31/43	6th Bn (105) 135th Bn* (105) 136th Bn* (155) 140th Bn (105)	117th Engineer Bn 112th Medical Bn 37th Recon Troop 37th QM Bn (Co) 37th Signal Co	15 Oct 40 Inducted into Federal service at Columbus, OH	26 May to 11 Jun 42 to Fiji then reached Guadalcanal 5 Apr 43 for training
38th IN, KY, & WV NG	149th (KYNG) 150th (WVNG) to 10 Feb 42 151st (INNG) 152d (INNG)	138th Bn* (105) 139th Bn* (105) 150th Bn* (155) 163d Bn (105)	113th Engineer Bn 113th Medical Bn 38th Recon Troop 38th QM Bn (Co) 38th Signal Co	17 Jan 41. Inducted into Federal service at Indianapolis, IN	31 Dec 43 to 21 Jan 44 to Hawaii; 23 Jul 44 landed at Oro Bay, New Guinea for training
40th CA, NV, & UT NG	159th (CANG) to 9/29/41 160th (CANG) [with 27th Inf Div 1 Sep 42 – 30 Oct 42 only] 184th (CANG) to 16 Jun 42 185th (CANG) 108th (NYNG) from 1 Sep 42 165th (NYNG) [1 Sep 42 to 30 Oct 42 only]	143d Bn* (105) 164th Bn (105) 213th Bn (105) 222d Bn* (155)	115th Engineer Bn 115th Medical Bn 40th Recon Troop 40th QM Bn (Co) 40th Signal Co	3 Mar 41. Inducted into Federal service at Los Angeles, CA	23 Aug to 1 Sep 42 to Hawaii; 20–31 Dec 43 to Guadalcanal for training; 23–28 Apr 44 to New Britain for security duties to 28 Nov 44; elements relieved 112th Cavalry at Arawe, Bismarks
41st WA, OR, ID, & MT NG	161st (WANG) detached 23 Jul 42 relieved 3 Aug 42 162d (ORNG) 163d (MTNG) 186th (ORNG)	146th Bn* (105) 167th Bn (105) 205th Bn (105) 218th Bn* (155)	116th Engineer Bn 116th Medical Bn 41st Recon Troop 41st QM Bn (Co) 41st Signal Co	16 Sep 40. Inducted into Federal service at Portland, OR	19 Mar to 13 May 42 to Australia
42d	222d Infantry 232d Infantry 242d Infantry	232d Bn (105) 392d Bn (105) 402d Bn (105) 542d Bn (155)	142d Engineer Bn 122d Medical Bn 42d Recon Troop 42d QM Bn (Co) 42d Signal Co	14 Jul 43. Activated at Camp Gruber, OK	6–18 Jan 45 to southern France
43d ME, VT, CT, & RI NG	102d (CTNG) to 19 Feb 42 103d (MENG) 169th (CTNG) 172d (VTNG)	103d Bn* (105) 152d Bn* (105) 169th Bn (105) 192d Bn (155)	118th Engineer Bn 118th Medical Bn 43d Recon Troop 43d QM Bn (Co) 43d Signal Co	24 Feb 41. Inducted into Federal service at Hartford, CT	1–22 Oct 42 to New Zealand except 172d Inf which lost its equipment at Espiritu Santo when *President Coolidge* struck a mine, 26 Oct 42

Jun 43, 148th Infantry landed in the Russell Islands and 145th Infantry landed on New Georgia. Most of the division was in action by 7 Jul 43. 147th Infantry fought on Guadalcanal from 4 Nov 42 while detached but not yet relieved from the 37th Division.	PA-6, PA-9	TBC: 5,960 KIA: 1,094 WIA: 4,861 (250) POW: 1 (0) MIA: 4 (4)	San Jose, Philippines
16 Dec 44 landed on Leyte; in action the same day	PA-5, PA-9	TBC: 3,464 KIA: 645 WIA: 2,814 (139) POW: 0 MIA: 5 (1)	Manila, Philippines
9 Jan 45 160th & 105th Infantry landed in Baybay–Lingayen area; full division in action by about 23 Jan 45	PA-7, PA-9	TBC: 3,025 KIA: 645 WIA: 2,814 (139) POW: 0 MIA: 5 (1)	Negros, Philippines
27 Dec 42, 163d Infantry reached New Guinea; in action by 8 Jan 43; whole division in action by mid Feb 43	PA-3, PA-5, PA-9	TBC: 4,260 KIA: 614 WIA: 2,407 (134) POW: 1 (0) MIA: 3 (0)	Zamboanga, Mindanao, Philippines
Adv. detachment reached Marseilles 9 Dec 44; whole division in action by 14 Feb 45	EU-4, EU-6	TBC: 3,971 KIA: 553 WIA: 2,212 (85) POW: 1,175 (14) MIA: 31 (3)	Wertheim, Germany
17-28 Feb 43 to Guadalcanal then Russell Islands & New Georgia Jun–Jul 43; 172d Inf rejoined 29 Jun 43; division in action on New Georgia (Munda Trail) 6 Jul 43	PA-4, PA-5, PA-6, PA-9	TBC: 6,026 KIA: 1,128 WIA: 4,887 (278) POW: 2 (0) MIA: 9 (8)	Cabanatuan, Philippines

44th NY & NJ NG	71st (NYNG) 113th (NJNG) to 2/16/42 114th (NJNG) 174th (NYNG) to 1/27/43 324th Inf from 1 Feb 43	156th Bn* (105) 157th Bn* (155) 217th Bn (105) 220th Bn (105)	63d Engineer Bn 119th Medical Bn 44th Recon Troop 44th QM Bn (Co) 44th Signal Co	16 Sep 40. Inducted into Federal service at Trenton, NJ	5–15 Sep 44 to France (Cherbourg) 20 Jul 45 arrived at NYC
45th AZ, CO, NM, & OK NG	157th (CONG) 158th (AZNG) to 11 Feb 42 179th (OKNG) 180th (OKNG)	158th Bn* (105) 160th Bn* (105) 171st Bn (105) 189th Bn (155)	120th Engineer Bn 120th Medical Bn 45th Recon Troop 45th QM Bn (Co) 45th Signal Co	16 Feb 40. Inducted into Federal service at Oklahoma City, OK	3–22 Jun 43 to N Africa
63d	253d Infantry 254th Infantry 255th Infantry	718th Bn (155) 861st Bn (105) 862d Bn (105) 863d Bn (105)	263d Engineer Bn 363d Medical Bn 63d Recon Troop 63d QM Bn (Co) 63d Signal Co	15 Jun 43. Activated at Camp Blanding, FL	5–14 Jun 45 to France; advance element (TF Harris) reached Marseilles 8 Dec 44
65th	259th Infantry 260th Infantry 261st Infantry	720th Bn (155) 867th Bn (105) 868th Bn (105) 869th Bn (105)	265th Engineer Bn 365th Medical Bn 65th Recon Troop 65th QM Bn (Co) 565th Signal Co	16 Aug 43. Activated at Camp Shelby, MS	10–21 Jan 45 to France (Le Havre)
66th	262d Infantry 263d Infantry 264th Infantry	721st Bn (155) 870th Bn (105) 871st Bn (105) 872d Bn (105)	266th Engineer Bn 366th Medical Bn 66th Recon Troop 66th QM Bn (Co) 566th Signal Co	15 Apr 43. Activated at Camp Blanding, FL	1–12 Dec 44 to UK; torpedoed en route to France (762 KIA) losing much equipment
69th	271st Infantry 272d Infantry 273d Infantry	724th Bn (155) 879th Bn (105) 880th Bn (105) 881st Bn (105)	265th Engineer Bn 365th Medical Bn 65th Recon Troop 65th QM Bn (Co) 565th Signal Co	15 May 43 Activated at Camp Shelby, MS	1–12 Dec 44 to UK
70th	274th Infantry 275th Infantry 276th Infantry	725th Bn (155) 882d Bn (105) 883d Bn (105) 884th Bn (105)	270th Engineer Bn 370th Medical Bn 70th Recon Troop 70th QM Bn (Co) 570th Signal Co	15 Jun 43. Activated at Camp Adair, OR	8–18 Jan 45 to Marseilles but the three infantry regiments arrived 10–15 Dec 44
71st (Light Infantry Div. (Pack, Jungle) until 26 May 44)	5th Infantry 14th Infantry 66th Infantry	564th Bn (155) 607th Bn (105) 608th Bn (105) 609th Bn (105)	271st Engineer Bn 371st Medical Bn 71st Recon Troop 251st QM Co 571st Signal Co	15 Jul 43. Activated at Camp Carson, CO	26 Jan to 6 Feb 45 to Le Havre, France
75th	289th Infantry 290th Infantry 291st Infantry	730th Bn (155) 897th Bn (105) 898th Bn (105) 899th Bn (105)	275th Engineer Bn 375th Medical Bn 75th Recon Troop 75th QM Bn (Co) 575th Signal Co	15 Apr 43. Activated at Fort Leonard Wood, MO	14–22 Nov 44 to UK then landed at Le Havre and Rouen, France 13 Dec 44

23–25 Oct 44 in action near Lunneville; then at Aachen and the Vosges	EU-2, EU-4, EU-6	TBC: 5,655 KIA: 1,038 WIA: 4,209 (168) POW: 308 (5) MIA: 100 (4)	Camp Chaffee, AR
10 Jul 43 assaulted Scoglitti, Sicily	IT-1, IT-2, IT-3, IT-4, EU-3, EU-4, EU-5, EU-6	TBC: 20,993 KIA: 3,547 WIA: 14,441 (533) POW: 2,527 (15) MIA: 478 (65)	Munich, Germany
Division in action by 17 Feb 45; advance element (TF Harris) in action from 22 Dec 44	EU-4, EU-6	TBC: 4,504 KIA: 861 WIA: 3,326 (113) POW: 219 (1) MIA: 98 (5)	Bad Mergentheim, Germany
9 Mar 45	EU-4, EU-6	TBC: 1,230 KIA: 233 WIA: 927 (27) POW: 67 (0) MIA: 3 (0)	Linz, Austria
25 Dec 44 landed at Cherbourg; from 29 Dec 44 used to besiege St Nazaire & Lorient until 8 May 45	EU-2	TBC: 1,452 KIA: 795 WIA: 636 (5) POW: 21 (0) MIA: 0	Chateaubriant, France
24 Jan 45 landed at Le Havre; in action by 26 Feb 45	EU-4, EU-6	TBC: 1,506 KIA: 341 WIA: 1,146 (42) POW: 10 (0) MIA: 9 (1)	Naumhof, Germany
From 3 Feb 45; as TF Herren the three infantry regts were in action from 28 Dec 44	EU-4, EU-6	TBC: 3,919 KIA: 755 WIA: 2,713 (79) POW: 397 (11) MIA: 54 (2)	Frankfurt, Germany
11 Mar 45	EU-4, EU-6	TBC: 1,114 KIA: 243 WIA: 843 (35) POW: 19 (0) MIA: 9 (1)	Wels, Austria
23 Dec 44	EU-4, EU-5, EU-6	TBC: 4,324 KIA: 817 WIA: 3,314 (111) POW: 116 (4) MIA: 77 (0)	Werdohl, Germany

76th	304th Infantry	302d Bn (105)	301st Engineer Bn	15 Jun 42.	10–20 Dec 44 to UK;
	395th Infantry	355th Bn (105)	301st Medical Bn	Activated at	landed at Le Havre,
	417th Infantry	364th Bn (155)	76th Recon Troop	Fort George	France 12 Jan 45
		901st Bn (105)	76th QM Bn (Co)	G. Meade,	
			76th Signal Co	MD	
77th	305th Infantry	304th Bn (105)	302d Engineer Bn	25 Mar 42.	24–30 Mar 44 to
	306th Infantry	305th Bn (105)	302d Medical Bn	Activated at	Hawaii; arrived
	307th Infantry	306th Bn (105)	77th Recon Troop	Fort Jackson, SC	Eniwetok 17 Jul 44
		902d Bn (155)	77th QM Bn (Co)		
			77th Signal Co		
78th	309th Infantry	307th Bn (105)	303d Engineer Bn	15 Aug 42.	14–25 Oct 44 to UK;
	310th Infantry	308th Bn (105)	303d Medical Bn	Activated at	landed in France
	311th Infantry	309th Bn (155)	78th Recon Troop	Camp Butner,	22 Nov 44
		903d Bn (105)	78th QM Bn (Co)	NC	
			78th Signal Co		
79th	313th Infantry	310th Bn (105)	304th Engineer Bn	15 Jun 42.	7–16 Apr 44 to UK
	314th Infantry	311th Bn (105)	304th Medical Bn	Activated at	
	315th Infantry	312th Bn (155)	79th Recon Troop	Camp Pickett, VA	
		904th Bn (105)	79th QM Bn (Co)		
			79th Signal Co		
80th	317th Infantry	313th Bn (105)	305th Engineer Bn	15 Jul 42	1–7 Jul 44 to UK
	318th Infantry	314th Bn (105)	305th Medical Bn	Activated at	
	319th Infantry	315th Bn (155)	80th Recon Troop	Camp Forrest, TN	
		905th Bn (105)	80th QM Bn (Co)		
			80th Signal Co		
81st	321st Infantry	316th Bn (105)	306th Engineer Bn	15 Jun 42.	3–6 Jul 44 to Hawaii;
	322d Infantry	317th Bn (105)	306th Medical Bn	Activated at	reached Guadalcanal
	323d Infantry	318th Bn (155)	81st Recon Troop	Camp Rucker, AL	24 Aug 44
		906th Bn (105)	81st QM Bn (Co)		
			81st Signal Co		
83d	329th Infantry	322d Bn (105)	308th Engineer Bn	15 Aug 42.	6–16 Apr 44 to UK
	330th Infantry	323d Bn (105)	308th Medical Bn	Activated at	
	331st Infantry	324th Bn (155)	83d Recon Troop	Camp Atterbury,	
		908th Bn (105)	83d QM Bn (Co)	IN	
			83d Signal Co		
84th	333d Infantry	325th Bn (105)	309th Engineer Bn	15 Oct 42	20 Sep to 4 Oct 44
	334th Infantry	326th Bn (105)	309th Medical Bn	Activated at	to UK; landed across
	335th Infantry	327th Bn (155)	84th Recon Troop	Camp Howze,	Omaha Beach
		909th Bn (105)	84th QM Bn (Co)	TX	1 Nov 44
			84th Signal Co		
85th	337th Infantry	328th Bn (105)	310th Engineer Bn	15 May 42	24 Dec 43 to
	338th Infantry	329th Bn (105)	310th Medical Bn	Activated at	2 Jan 44 to
	339th Infantry	403d Bn (155)	85th Recon Troop	Camp Shelby,	Casablanca North
		910th Bn (105)	85th QM Bn (Co)	MS	Africa
			85th Signal Co		
86th	341st Infantry	331st Bn (105)	311th Engineer Bn	15 Dec 42.	19 Feb to 1 Mar 45
	342d Infantry	332d Bn (105)	311th Medical Bn	Activated at	to France
	343d Infantry	404th Bn (155)	86th Recon Troop	Camp Howze,	Returned to NYC
		911th Bn (105)	86th QM Bn (Co)	TX	17 Jun 45
			86th Signal Co		

25 Jan 45	EU-4, EU-5, EU-6	TBC: 2,395 KIA: 433 WIA: 1,811 (90) POW: 141 (0) MIA: 10 (0)	Limbach, Germany
21–22 Jul 44, landed on Guam	PA-9, PA-10, PA-11	TBC: 7,461 KIA: 1,449 WIA: 5,935 (401) POW: 1 (0) MIA: 76 (7)	Cebu, Philippines
12 Dec 44	EU-4, EU-5, EU-6	TBC: 8,146 KIA: 1,427 WIA: 6,103 (198) POW: 385 (4) MIA: 231 (5)	Dillenberg, Germany
14 Jun 44 landed across Utah Beach; attacked towards Cherbourg 19 Jun 44	EU-1, EU-2, EU-4, EU-5, EU-6	TBC: 15,203 KIA: 2,476 WIA: 10,971 (467) POW: 1,186 (5) MIA: 570 (16)	Neheim, Germany
3 Aug 44 landed across Utah Beach; in action by 8 Aug 44	EU-2, EU-4, EU-5, EU-6	TBC: 17,087 KIA: 3,038 WIA: 12,484 (442) POW: 1,077 (8) MIA: 488 (12)	Pichlwany, Austria
7 Sep 44 assaulted Angaur, Palau Islands	PA-9, PA-10	TBC: 2,314 KIA: 366 WIA: 1,942 (149) POW: 0 MIA: 6 (2)	Leyte, Philippines
19 Jun 44 landed across Omaha Beach; in action by 4 Jul 44	EU-1, EU-2, EU-4, EU-5, EU-6	TBC: 15,910 KIA: 3,161 WIA: 11,807 (459) POW: 663 (6) MIA: 279 (11)	Wernigerode, Germany
12 Nov 44	EU-4, EU-5, EU-6	TBC: 7,260 KIA: 1,284 WIA: 5,098 (154) POW: 749 (13) MIA: 129 (17)	Salzwedel, Germany
15–27 Mar 44 landed at Naples; full division in action 10 Apr 44	IT-4, IT-5, IT-6	TBC: 8,744 KIA: 1,561 WIA: 6,314 (175) POW: 497 (3) MIA: 402 (36)	Fagianeria, Italy
29 Mar 45	EU-6	TBC: 785 KIA: 136 WIA: 618 (25) POW: 19 (0) MIA: 12 (0)	Camp Stoneman, CA

87th	345th Infantry	334th Bn (105)	312th Engineer Bn	15 Dec 42.	4–12 Nov 44 to UK;
	346th Infantry	335th Bn (155)	312th Medical Bn	Activated at	to France 5 Dec 44
	347th Infantry	346th Bn (105)	87th Recon Troop	Camp McCain,	Returned to NYC
		912th Bn (105)	87th QM Bn (Co)	MS	11 Jul 45
			87th Signal Co		
88th	349th Infantry	337th Bn (105)	313th Engineer Bn	15 Jul 42.	6–15 Dec 43 to
	350th Infantry	338th Bn (105)	313th Medical Bn	Activated at	Casablanca, N Africa
	351st Indantry	339th Bn (155)	88th Recon Troop	Camp Gruber,	
		913th Bn (105)	88th QM Bn (Co)	OK	
			88th Signal Co		
89th (Light Inf.	353d Infantry	340th Bn (105)	314th Engineer Bn	15 Jul 42.	10–21 Jan 45 to
Division (Truck)	354th Infantry	341st Bn (105)	314th Medical Bn	Activated at	Le Havre, France
until 15 Jun 44)	355th Infantry	563d Bn (155)	89th Recon Troop	Camp Carson,	
		914th Bn (105)	405th QM Co	CO	
			89th Signal Co		
90th (Motorized	357th Infantry	343d Bn (105)	315th Engineer Bn	25 Mar 42.	23 Mar to 4 Apr 44
Division	358th Infantry	344th Bn (105)	315th Medical Bn	Activated at	to UK
15 Sep 42 to	359th Infantry	345th Bn (155)	90th Recon Troop	Camp Barkeley,	
1 May 43)		915th Bn (105)	90th QM Bn (Co)	TX	
			90th Signal Co		
91st	361st Infantry	346th Bn (105)	316th Engineer Bn	15 Aug 42.	14–21 Apr 44 to
	362d Infantry	347th Bn (155)	316th Medical Bn	Activated at	N Africa
	363d Infantry	348th Bn (105)	91st Recon Troop	Camp White, OR	Returned to Hampton
		916th Bn (105)	91st QM Bn (Co)		Roads 10 Sep 45
			91st Signal Co		
92d (Colored)	365th Infantry (Cld)	597th Bn (105)	317th Engineer Bn	15 Oct 42.	17–22 Sep 44 to
	370th Infantry (Cld)	598th Bn (105)	317th Medical Bn	Activated at	Naples Italy; 370th
	371st Infantry (Cld)	599th Bn (105)	92d Recon Troop	Fort McClellan,	Infantry arrived
	366th Infantry (Cld)	600th Bn (155)	92d QM Bn (Co)	MD	1 Aug 44
	attached 21 Nov 44	all bns colored	92d Signal Co		
	to 25 Feb 45				
	442d Inf attached				
	from 30 Mar 45				
	473d Inf attached				
	from 24 Feb 45				
93d (Colored)	25th Infantry (Cld)	593d Bn (105)	318th Engineer Bn	15 May 42.	11 Jan to 5 Mar 44
	368th Infantry (Cld)	594th Bn (105)	318th Medical Bn	Activated at	moved by echelon to
	369th Infantry (Cld)	595th Bn (105)	93d Recon Troop	Fort Huachuca,	Guadalcanal
		596th Bn (155)	93d QM Bn (Co)	AZ	
		all bns colored	93d Signal Co		
94th	301st Infantry	301st Bn (105)	319th Engineer Bn	15 Sep 42.	6–11 Aug 44 to UK;
	302d Infantry	356th Bn (105)	319th Medical Bn	Activated at	landed across Utah
	376th Infantry	390th Bn (155)	94th Recon Troop	Fort Custer,	Beach, 8 Sep 44
		919th Bn (105)	94th QM Bn (Co)	MI	
			94th Signal Co		
95th	377th Infantry	358th Bn (105)	320th Engineer Bn	15 Jul 42.	10–17 Aug 44 to UK;
	378th Infantry	359th Bn (105)	320th Medical Bn	Activated at	landed in France
	379th Infantry	360th Bn (155)	95th Recon Troop	Camp Swift,	15 Sep 44
		920th Bn (105)	95th QM Bn (Co)	TX	Returned to Boston
			95th Signal Co		29 Jun 45

8 Dec 44 (at siege of Metz)	EU-4, EU-5, EU-6	TBC: 6,034 KIA: 1,154 WIA: 4,342 (141) POW: 429 (11) MIA: 109 (10)	Fort Benning, Georgia
6 Feb 44 arrived at Naples; in action at Mount Castellone 28 Feb 44	IT-4, IT-5, IT-6	TBC: 13,111 KIA: 2,298 WIA: 9,225 (258) POW: 647 (0) MIA: 941 (50)	Desenzano, Italy
12 Mar 45	EU-4, EU-6	TBC: 1,029 KIA: 292 WIA: 692 (33) POW: 40 (0) MIA: 5 (0)	Werdau, Germany
359th Inf. was at Utah Beach 6 Jun 44; full division landed 8 Jun, in action 10 Jun 44	EU-1, EU-2, EU-4, EU-5, EU-6	TBC: 19,200 KIA: 3,342 WIA: 14,306 (588) POW: 1,185 (7) MIA: 287 (14)	Eisenstein, Germany
361st Inf landed at Anzio 1 Jun 44; full division arrived 19 Jun, in action 13 Jul 44	IT-4, IT-5, IT-6	TBC: 8,744 KIA: 1,400 WIA: 6,748 (175 POW: 334 (2) MIA: 262 (4)	Angoris, Italy
370th Infantry in action from 2 3 Aug 44; full division in action from 6 Oct 44 365th Infantry became a replacement training center & 371st Infantry assigned to rear security duties by 3 Apr 45	IT-5, IT-6	TBC: 2,997 KIA: 548 WIA: 2,187 (68) POW: 56 (0) MIA: 206 (8)	Torre Del Lago, Italy
Division elements dispersed among Pacific islands for garrison, labor & mopping up duties; 25th Infantry saw limited action on Bougainville Apr 44	PA-5, PA-6, PA-7	TBC: 133 KIA: 12 WIA: 121 (5) POW: 0 MIA: 0	Morotai Island
16 Sep 44 besieged Lorient until 1 Jan 45; then to Saar–Moselle 7 Jan 45	EU-2, EU-4, EU-5, EU-6	TBC: 6,533 KIA: 1,009 WIA: 4,789 (147) POW: 619 (10) MIA: 116 (6)	Dusseldorf, Germany
19 Oct 44, in the Moselle River bridgehead south of Metz	EU-2, EU-4, EU-5, EU-6	TBC: 6,591 KIA: 1,205 WIA: 4,945 (167) POW: 380 (6) MIA: 61 (9)	Camp Shelby, MI

96th	381st Infantry 382d Infantry 383d Infantry	361st Bn (105) 362d Bn (105) 363d Bn (155) 921st Bn (105)	321st Engineer Bn 321st Medical Bn 96th Recon Troop 96th QM Bn (Co) 96th Signal Co	15 Aug 42. Activated at Camp Adair, OR	23–28 Jul 44 to Hawaii; to Eniwetok 15–28 Sep & Manus 28 Sep to 3 Oct 44
97th	303d Infantry 386th Infantry 387th Infantry	303d Bn (105) 365th Bn (105) 389th Bn (155) 922d Bn (105)	322d Engineer Bn 322d Medical Bn 97th Recon Troop 97th QM Bn (Co) 97th Signal Co	25 Feb 43. Activated at Camp Swift, TX	19 Feb to 1 Mar 45 to Le Havre, France Returned to NYC 26 Jun 45
98th	389th Infantry 390th Infantry 391st Infantry	367th Bn (105) 368th Bn (105) 369th Bn (155) 923d Bn (105)	323d Engineer Bn 323d Medical Bn 98th Recon Troop 98th QM Bn (Co) 98th Signal Co	15 Sep 42. Activated at Camp Breckinridge, KY	13–19 Apr 44 to Hawaii
99th	393d Infantry 394th Infantry 395th Infantry	370th Bn (105) 371st Bn (105) 372d Bn (155) 924th Bn (105)	324th Engineer Bn 324th Medical Bn 99th Recon Troop 99th QM Bn (Co) 99th Signal Co	15 Nov 42. Activated at Camp Van Dorn, MS	30 Sep to 10 Oct 44 to UK; landed at Le Havre, France 3 Nov 44
100th	397th Infantry 398th Infantry 399th Infantry	373d Bn (105) 374th Bn (105) 375th Bn (155) 925th Bn (105)	325th Engineer Bn 325th Medical Bn 100th Recon Troop 100th QM Bn (Co) 100th Signal Co	15 Nov 42. Activated at Fort Jackson, SC	6–20 Oct 44 to France (Marseilles)
102d	405th Infantry 406th Infantry 407th Infantry	379th Bn (105) 380th Bn (105) 381st Bn (155) 927th Bn (105)	327th Engineer Bn 327th Medical Bn 102d Recon Troop 102d QM Bn (Co) 102d Signal Co	15 Sep 42. Activated at Camp Maxey, TX	12–23 Sep 44 to Cherbourg, France
103d	409th Infantry 410th Infantry 411th Infantry	382d Bn (105) 383d Bn (105) 384th Bn (155) 928th Bn (105)	328th Engineer Bn 328th Medical Bn 103d Recon Troop 103d QM Bn (Co) 103d Signal Co	15 Nov 42. Activated at Camp Claiborne, LA	20 Oct 44 landed at Marseilles, France
104th	413th Infantry 414th Infantry 415th Infantry	385th Bn (105) 386th Bn (105) 387th Bn (155) 929th Bn (105)	329th Engineer Bn 329th Medical Bn 104th Recon Troop 104th QM Bn (Co) 104th Signal Co	15 Sep 42. Activated at Camp Adair, OR	27 Aug to 7 Sep 44 to France. Returned to NYC 3 Jul 45
106th	422d Infantry 423d Infantry 424th Infantry 3d Inf (att. 16 Mar 45) 159th (att 16 Mar 45)	589th Bn (105) 590th Bn (105) 591st Bn (105) 592d Bn (155)	81st Engineer Bn 331st Medical Bn 106th Recon Troop 106th QM Bn (Co) 106th Signal Co	15 Mar 43. Activated at Camp Jackson, SC	10–17 Nov 44 to UK landed in France 6 Dec 44
AMERICAL	132d (ILNG) 164th (NDNG) 182d (MANG)	221st Bn (155) 245th Bn (105) 246th Bn (105) 247th Bn (105)	57th Engineer Bn 121st Medical Bn 21st Recon Troop 121st QM Co 26th Signal Co	24 May 42. Organized on New Caledonia from TF 6814 and other units	Moved to Guadalcanal by echelon 12 Nov to 8 Dec 42

20 Oct 44, assaulted Leyte & Okinawa 1 Apr to 31 Jul 45; returned to Philippines	PA-9, PA-11	TBC: 8,812 KIA: 1,563 WIA: 7,181 (473) POW: 5 (0) MIA: 63 (2)	Mindoro, Philippines
4 Apr 45	EU-6	TBC: 979 KIA: 188 WIA: 721 (26) POW: 61 (0) MIA: 9 (1)	Fort Bragg, NC
Never in combat; landed in Japan 27 Sep 45	Pacific Theater (no campaigns)	TBC: 0 KIA: 0 WIA: 0 POW: 0 MIA: 0	Fort Hase, Hawaii
9 Nov 44, north of Monschau	EU-4, EU-5, EU-6	TBC: 6,553 KIA: 993 WIA: 4,177 (141) POW: 1,136 (21) MIA: 247 (13)	Pfeffenhausen, Germany
12 Nov 44 in the Vosges; advance elements were in action 1 Nov 44	EU-4, EU-5, EU-6	TBC: 5,038 KIA: 883 WIA: 3,539 (101) POW: 491 (8) MIA: 125 (5)	Goppingen, Germany
Entered combat in increments during 26-28 Oct 44 as attachments to other divisions	EU-4, EU-6	TBC: 4,922 KIA: 932 WIA: 3,668 (145) POW: 137 (0) MIA: 185 (11)	Gardelegen, Germany
9 Nov 44, fought in the Vosges	EU-4, EU-5, EU-6	TBC: 4,558 KIA: 720 WIA: 3,329 (101) POW: 421 (3) MIA: 88 (10)	Innsbruck, Austria
23 Oct 44 (in Belgium)	EU-2, EU-4, EU-6	TBC: 4,961 KIA: 971 WIA: 3,657 (143) POW: 237 (2) MIA: 96 (3)	Camp San Louis, Obispo, CA
11 Dec 44 422d & 423d Regts surrendered in the Ardennes, 19 Dec 44 Division largely destroyed 16–30 Dec 44; rebuilt but never fought again	EU-4, EU-5, EU-6	TBC: 8,627 KIA: 417 WIA: 1,278 (53) POW: 6,697 (197) MIA: 235 (26)	Bad Ems, Germany
164th Regt reached Guadalcanal 13 Oct, 182d 12 Nov, & 132d & Div HQ, 8 Dec 42.	PA-4, PA-6, PA-9	TBC: 4,050 KIA: 981 WIA: 3,052 (176) POW: 1 (0) MIA: 16 (11)	Cebu Island, Philippines

Notes:

(1) All infantry units are regiments. National Guard divisions initially had four, grouped into two infantry brigades numbered sequentially by division (for example, the 26th Division had the 51st and 52d Brigades and the 27th had the 53d and 54th, etc.). National Guard regiments are indicated by state of origin (CANG = California National Guard, etc.)

(2) All artillery units are battalions. Those marked with an asterisk (*) were regiments until Jan–Feb 1942.

(3) Until Jan–Feb 1942 National Guard divisions had engineer, medical and quartermaster regiments in lieu of battalions. They also had ordnance companies. The division counter intelligence detachment (added after July 15, 1943) had the same number as its parent division (except that the Americal Division had the 182d CI Detachment). Each division also received an ordnance light maintenance company after September 15, 1942. This unit received a number equal to that of its parent division plus "700." Thus, for example, the 1st Infantry Division would have the 701st Ordnance Light Maintenance Company. The only exceptions were the 700th Ordnance Light Maintenance Company in the 45th Infantry Division, the 714th in the 89th Division and the 721st in the Americal Division.

(4) Port of embarkation in the Continental United States (CONUS) and initial overseas destination are indicated. If the division returned to CONUS prior to August 1945 the dates of this are also given.

(5) Date of arrival in a combat theater (as a division) and date of first combat (if different from the arrival date) are given.

(6) Campaigns are indicated by the following key:

EU-1 Normandy (6 Jun to 24 Jul 44)
EU-2 Northern France (25 Jul to 14 Sep 44)
EU-3 Southern France (15 Aug to 14 Sep 44)
EU-4 Rhineland (15 Sep 44 to 21 Mar 45)
EU-5 Ardennes–Alsace (16 Dec 44 to 25 Jan 45)
EU-6 Central Europe (22 Mar to 11 May 45)
NA-1 Algeria/French Morocco (8–11 Nov 42)
NA-2 Tunisia (17 Nov 42 to 13 May 43)
PA-1 Central Pacific (7 Dec 41 to 6 Dec 43)
PA-2 Aleutians (3 Jun 42 to 24 Aug 43)
PA-3 Papua New Guinea (23 Jul 42 to 23 Jan 43)
PA-4 Guadalcanal (7 Aug 42 to 21 Feb 43)
PA-5 New Guinea (24 Jan 43 to 31 Dec 44)
PA-6 Northern Solomons (22 Feb 43 to 21 Nov 44)
PA-7 Bismark Archipelago (15 Dec 43 to 27 Nov 44)
PA-8 E. Mandates (31 Jan to 14 Jun 44)
PA-9 Leyte, Luzon and Southern Philippines (17 Oct 44 to 4 Jul 45)
PA-10 Western Pacific (15 Jun 44 to 2 Sep 45)
PA-11 Ryukyus (26 Mar to 2 Jul 45)
IT-1 Sicily (9 Jul to 17 Aug 43)
IT-2 Naples–Foggia (9 Sep 43 to 21 Jan 44)
IT-3 Anzio (22 Jan to 24 May 44)
IT-4 Rome–Arno (22 Jan to 9 Sep 44)
IT-5 North Apennines (10 Sep 44 to 4 Apr 45)
IT-6 Po Valley (5 Apr to 8 May 45)

(7) Casualties are only for elements organic to the division; battle casualties of attached and supporting units (excluding air) would on average add about 20 percent to the total. Non-battle losses would amount to as much as 100 percent of battle casualties but a much smaller percentage would be fatal. TBC = total battle casualties; KIA = killed in action; WIA = wounded in action (the number who died of their wounds appears in brackets; these are deaths in addition to KIA); about a third of the WIA were evacuated to the United States, the rest recovered (and returned to duty) in theater; POW = personnel captured/interned, including those who died (in brackets) and those later repatriated; MIA = missing in action; it includes personnel not recovered and subsequently presumed dead (in brackets) and those who subsequently returned to duty.

(8) The divisions that returned from Europe to the United States prior to August 1945 were en route to the Pacific Theater to take part in the invasion of Japan.

(9) 147th Infantry detached on 6 Apr 42 but not formally relieved until 31 Jul 43.

Index